You REALLLLY don't want to miss out on the BUNDLE.

Value: $54.90

Bundle Price: $26.99
What's Included?

- 🌲 100 gorgeous, realistic 3-Part Montessori Cards
- 🌲 Various animal life cycle posters and worksheets
- 🌲 Memory Statement Cards for all 3 levels
- 🌲 Convenient printable book lists, "At-A-Glance" pages, and handicraft menu
- 🌲 Gorgeous poetry cards with related art
- 🌲 Stunning posters
- 🌲 French and Spanish Flashcards
- 🌲 Nature Collection Journal (Top Seller!)
- 🌲 Gorgeous Bird Observation Collection and MORE!

©2019 Erin Elizabeth Cox
All Rights Reserved.
Do not copy, reprint, alter, or redistribute in any way.
For use in home settings only. Contact erin@lifeabundantlyblog.com for use in classrooms or co-ops.
FONT: Print Clearly by Blue Vinyl via www.FontSpace.com

ISBN: 9781798781579
The Gentle + Classical Press
www.LifeAbundantlyBlog.com   www.GentleClassical.com

Gentle + Classical
Nature

Confidently guide your child in exploring God's Creation using a gentle, natural method of early education.

Term 1: Inland Waterways and Forests
Ages: 4 years - 2nd grade

For Isabella and Kali- without your support, your role as guinea pigs, and your hours of loving on and wrestling with your brothers, this program would not exist.

For Daxton and Kolton- I pray that the seeds sown into your heart will leave an indelible imprint on your lives and an undying reverence for your Creator.

Danny- You are the perfect balance to my crazy obsessions, always encouraging and loving me without fail. You're everything. Always.

Amanda- You are an encouragement, blessing, and my lifelong partner-in-crime. You are a selfless servant who gives generously without a second thought. I'm so grateful to have such an amazing big sister!

Hayley- You are my constant sounding board, homeschooling spirit animal, and never-failing counselor and friend. Thank you for being YOU!

Mama- I pray this work honors your memory. Thank your for teaching us what it looks like to live life abundantly.

Ginny, Carina, and Amanda- Thank you for helping me find all the errors of my way ;-) and volunteering your precious time to make this program come to fruition!

Table of Contents

Page	Topic
2	**Part 1**
4	Welcome Letter
8	Preparing Our Hearts + Minds as Teachers
11	Scope and Sequence for Gentle + Classical Nature- 3 Terms
14	What are "attainments?"
16	List of Formidable Attainments issued by Charlotte Mason
19	How to Plan + Schedule; **"Quick Start" Guide**
25	Levels, Explained (integrating older children)
27	Attainments (detailed) + HOW do we accomplish them?
38	Purpose + Importance of Memorization
43	Alignment with Gentle + Classical Preschool program
44	**Part 2**
45	Unit 1- Amphibians
53	Unit 2- Freshwater Fish
57	Unit 3- Aquatic Arthropods
61	Unit 4- Freshwater Waterbirds
66	Unit 5- Freshwater Mammals
70	Unit 6- Reptiles
76	Unit 7- Inland Birds
81	Unit 8- Forest Animals
86	Unit 9- Butterflies
92	Unit 10- Bees
98	Unit 11- Arachnids
103	Unit 12- Worms
108	**Appendix**

IMPORTANT

This curriculum is composed of two parts:

PART 1: Introduction, scope and sequence, scheduling, and detailed teacher guidance.

PART 2: Curriculum Content

If the philosophies of Charlotte Mason and Classical Education are new to you, if possible, please take the time to read through Part 1 in advance of beginning Gentle + Classical Nature. I challenge you to read through it at least twice as well as to prayerfully consider reading Volume 1: Home Education by Charlotte Mason for yourself. You'll be immensely blessed.

NOTE: All links, suggested books, and materials found in this program can be found "clickable" on ONE page at www.GentleClassical.com.

Part 1

Welcome

Welcome, friend, to Gentle + Classical Nature from Life, Abundantly!

As you begin to invest time and energy into exploring this program and all that it offers, I want to share the heart behind it and the motivation for the months of work that went into developing it. As a homeschool mama of 4 children, a student of many educational philosophies, and an ardent enthusiast of "the best way," I've come to firmly and deeply settle my heart and practices into a method of education that could be loosely called "Classical-Charlotte Mason."

I'd love to impart a brief overview of how I've come to teach the way that I have in our home, so that you will understand my perspective. As almost universal idealists, most homeschool mothers whom I know love to peruse the buffet of homeschool methods and opportunities set before them and carefully select those aspects that settle most readily into their personal idea of "what is best" alongside "what is best for this particular child." We each come into our home education careers with ideals, notions, goals, and visions for our days. As a whole, we tend to be "samplers" and arriving at an eclectic mix of various philosophies is certainly not unique to me. This typical "sampling" summary describes my own adventure in home education perfectly.

The idea of blending modern aspects of classical education together with the timeless philosophy of Charlotte Mason (with splashes of Montessori thrown in) is not an uncommon homeschool philosophy. Classical education, with its trivium, quadrivium, clear stepping stones of developmental progression, and memorization tactics imparts a systematic ease that seems readily adaptable into almost any homeschool environment. The Montessori method, with its gentleness, natural simplicity, and play-based learning appeals to our desire for simple times, family togetherness, and meeting our children right where they are. Most whom become acquainted with Charlotte Mason love many aspects of her philosophy and quickly usher several tools from her methods into their own homeschool such as: narration, copywork, handicrafts, and living books.

Over 7 years of home education, I've come to realize that the appeal of these specific aspects of a Charlotte Mason education often comes from the perspective that a full Charlotte Mason education is too complicated, too expensive, or too antiquated to be applicable today. The fact that her original works are written in Victorian English makes her methods seem a little too distant or complicated for many of us. Furthermore, this type of education can seem foreign to those of us educated in traditional American classrooms. Lastly, while some Charlotte Mason enthusiasts might argue wholeheartedly with me, the full feast of the Mason education can seem incredibly daunting to schedule into our days.

One of the most important motivating factors behind Gentle + Classical Nature (GCN) is my own desire to better understand and implement much of Miss Mason's philosophy in our home in an incredibly practical way, without becoming overwhelmed by schedules that don't fit our particular lifestyle or compromising my own personal educational convictions where they may depart from Miss Mason's. While I can see the value and beauty in being a Charlotte Mason "purist" (and I always use that term in the most positive light possible), I am not one. While I agree wholeheartedly with much of Miss Mason's philosophy and writings, I've not come away from reading her works in complete agreement every single time. I don't state this to over share my own personal opinions, but simply to say that I am not a purist, and therefore this curriculum is not purely built around Mason's philosophy alone. (Though I will add that I have only disagreed with her, thus far, less than a handful of times!) Furthermore, my position is that Charlotte Mason was herself a classical educator, in the purest sense of the word, though her applications of classical education do not necessarily align with some modern aspects of the classical education movement. (A great book to learn more about this subject is Consider This by Karen Glass.)

I believe I've consumed a drop in the bucket of all there is to learn about her philosophy and of education in general. It is my heart's desire to be a lifelong student of home education, and I have much to learn. But my short 7 years of pursuing knowledge and experience about homeschooling has led me to one strong and resolute belief: There is NO **ONE** WAY to homeschool "perfectly." To be more clear, there is "no one way" and also, there is no such thing as a perfect homeschool.

I believe that the most beautiful aspect of home education is the freedom to adapt, co-mingle, and extract any particular practice from any available homeschool method and place it into our own unique homeschool. One of the most beautiful, and yes— overwhelming— aspects of education at home is the freedom that we have to choose, manipulate, expand, simplify, and blend any of the vast numbers of educational philosophies that are available to create our own unique approach. Each homeschool family can be truly one-of-a-kind! In this volume, that is what I've ventured to do: handpick the best of several various philosophies and co-mingle them to become my own.

Hear me clearly, friend, as you come to know this author's heart through her words: the ONLY correct philosophy of education for your homeschool is the one that the Holy Spirit has called you to. As I share my perspectives, ideals, and methods with you alongside much input from Charlotte Mason, I want you to know that we are not your greatest advisors. The God that created you, created your child, and gifted him/her to you to parent/educate is.

The freedom found in homeschooling that can be so overwhelming becomes intrinsically perfect when we ask for and allow the Holy Spirit to guide us. In this guide, you will find advice and encouragement in educating your children in observing, collecting, cherishing, and identifying nature and the wonders of creation gifted all around us. The ideas that I present to you will be beautiful, peaceful, wholesome, and God-honoring. However, that does not mean this is THE perfect curriculum or that something out there would not be better suited for your personality, your child's learning style, your family's budget, or your family's schedule. There is no "one way."

This curriculum has been created to be the perfect nature study and science program for **my family**, based on our needs, preferences, and beliefs. That doesn't mean that it's a "one-size-fits-all" solution. Those actually don't exist, and it's probably one reason why you homeschool! However, as I have prayed through its creation, I fully and profoundly believe that Gentle + Classical Nature will be an excellent tool for many families who love God, are inspired to deeply and profoundly be acquainted with His Creation, want to honor their child's natural developmental rhythm, and need practical, encouraging help in ordering their days to reach the vision they've cultivated for their homeschool.

So whether you are a new homeschooler or veteran, a Charlotte Mason purist, Classicist, or everything all mixed up in-between, I hope that you'll be blessed by walking with me through this program. We are one community, pursuing the same ideal: to know God fully, to obey him eagerly, and to sufficiently and wholly make him known to our children, for His Glory.

If I needed to solidify the purpose of Gentle + Classical Nature in one (long) statement, it would be this:

Through the exploration of God's Creation, we shall sufficiently and wholly introduce wonder into our children's hearts and minds so that their appetite is whetted to continually wonder at, pursue knowledge of, and cultivate intimacy with both creation and its Creator, in a natural, developmentally appropriate manner that is practical in scope and application for the modern homeschool family.

Home education is a task of overwhelming patience— much like our overall journey of parenthood which begins at conception and ends when we draw our last breath. These long days at home with little ones, big ones, and everyone in between mesh themselves into months and years filled with memories and purpose, ultimately culminating into a life well-lived as we sow truth, beauty, goodness, character, and virtue into the very fabric of our children's souls. This, sweet friend, is hard and holy work as we journey through sacred terrain. Let us never forget the legacy building task set before us and the hallowed ground that we stand upon.

May God bless you, keep you, encourage and inspire you in all that you do.

Jesus in. Joy out.

In Christ,
Erin

P.S. While this curriculum was written with the intention of being "open-and-go" on a day-to-day basis, I encourage you to read all the information preceding the lessons. The many pages written before we begin Unit 1 are meant to equip you to receive the most benefit possible, as mother and teacher.

Preparing Our Hearts and Minds as Teachers

At first glance (and possibly second!), this program may seem intimidating. There are many parts to it, and honestly, it's very different from how most of us were educated. It's SO different that there is a learning curve for us as Mama/Teachers that we have to tackle head-on.

Admittedly, most programs don't require (BEG) that you read an entire book before utilizing them. While that's truly in your own hands (**and the program can certainly be used if you don't**), this author asks you to take the time to read Charlotte Mason's Volume 1: Home Education for yourself then asks you to read through Part 1 of this program at least twice before you begin.

Why? Because, for most of us, we are very much used to (and looking for) "open and go." That's my typical scouting process for new curriculum: "Is it OPEN AND GO?" I 1000% get it, friend. We have limited time and many of us have several children, in various grades, with different learning styles to consider. **However, what I'm imploring of you here is something that will inherently affect how you educate every single child in your home, regardless of their ages or abilities, from this point forward.**

As you grow in understanding of this "classical/CM" method, this program becomes very "open and go" on a daily and weekly basis. Aside from procuring books and ordering a few supplies for term projects, your week-to-week planning won't be stressful or cumbersome at all. I personally feel like this will be due to your diligence and faithfulness in fully preparing your own heart and mind prior to stepping into the program.

In planning for your child's year of nature exploration, you'll want to take time to plan for your own education as well. One of the most exciting aspects of home education is the ability to enrich our own thought lives, expand our own understanding, and learn new things about how God made us and designed us to learn! You will reap a 100-fold bounty in your own heart and in your child's education by investing your time into this preparation.

Here are a few tips to take into consideration during your "planning phase" of using GCN:
- Rather than seek out a "summary" of Charlotte Mason's ideas (and there are some great ones), if you are educating a child under the age of 6, nothing will surpass the beauty and clarity of reading Miss Mason's OWN words about this season in Volume 1: Home Education.
- My personal edition (and there are many) is from "The Home Education Series" published by Living Books Press and has been formatted to match the original printings (and page numbers). This will be very helpful as I direct you to certain pages throughout Part 1 of this curriculum to read Miss Mason's instructions in various skills, where they are too lengthy for me to include here. This book is listed in the Appendix on the book list.
- Even if time doesn't allow for you to read it in full before beginning GCN, you will want to have it on hand, nonetheless. As mentioned above, it is often cited, and is therefore an indispensable resource in implementing GCN. If you can't read the full book, reading through page 233 will give

you the vast majority of insight you need for a child under the age of 6. For children over 6, I really encourage you to read the whole volume.

- There is also a FREE online version, with original page citations, that will roughly align with citations in this book. That link can also be found in the Suggested Resources of the Appendix.
- Obviously, the homeschool police will not show up if you don't read the book first! You can likely skip into the curriculum if you are very enthusiastic to begin, then reference back as needed. My entire hope is that you will have all the tools and information readily at your disposal so that your year of Gentle + Classical Nature is overflowing with goodness and ease for yourself and your child.

Scope + Sequence Program Structure

Gentle + Classical Nature is composed of 36 units of work, divided into 3 terms. They are:

TERM 1: INLAND WATERWAYS AND FORESTS
TERM 2: COASTAL WOODLANDS AND OCEANS (releasing fall 2019)
TERM 3: DOWN ON THE FARM AND AROUND THE WORLD (releasing winter 2019)

In this volume, **Term 1: Inland Waterways and Forests**, you'll find the following 12 topics:

1. Amphibians
2. Freshwater Fish
3. Aquatic Arthropods
4. Freshwater Birds
5. Freshwater Mammals
6. Reptiles
7. Inland Birds
8. Forest Animals
9. Insects (Butterflies)
10. Insects (Bees)
11. Arachnids
12. Worms

There are two general "sections" in each unit: **Attainments and Nature Focus.**

We will be walking through a process of meeting each of the "attainments" (described in detail in the next section) in a very clear and natural methodology as we also explore various organisms and habitats with intentionality and depth through each unit. You will see a clear division between these "sections" in each unit, yet they inherently flow together. They are done this way so that you can choose any of the following 4 ways to use this program:

1. Focus on the attainments alone.
2. Utilize the nature focus only.
3. Use the entire program as a "menu" to choose books, activities, or attainments.
4. Do everything as outlined and scheduled.

> **STOP:** Time to make a decision! Once you've read through Part 1, you will need to evaluate HOW you want to use this program as outlined here.

In each unit, throughout all 3 terms, you will find the same consistent format and sections:

<u>Unit Overview</u>- This section defines any special purpose inherent to each particular unit, provides a brief overview of how the levels may differ, and may include general notes of encouragement.

Nature Nuggets- This section contains direct links to a few websites I found that shared information that was perfect for children and very interesting. Due to copyright, I can't copy and paste this information for you. However, you may access one page of all clickable links at www.GentleClassical.com (big black button that says "Nature Nugget Links"). I highly encourage you to read these resources (or any other resource you find easy to access) so that you are equipped with interesting "nuggets" of information to share with your students, at just the right time.

Teacher Notes- Planning notes for each unit are outlined here, as well as a variety of ideas for explorations, projects, and activities related to the unit's focus. If I've found products or resources online that I feel like would be a perfect fit, I'll share those here as well. I'll also include any important "heads-up" that you may need for supplies or preparation for upcoming units.

Unit Attainments- In this section, specific steps for accomplishing each "attainment" is detailed along with its own checklist. Each unit will include visiting a Walk/View or "Body of Water," poem recitation, handicraft practice, identifying plants or birds, along with reviewing what's already been accomplished in previous units. Each of the attainments will be discussed in deep detail shortly in this introductory section of the book. Furthermore a planning sheet is included in the appendix.

Unit At-A-Glance- This section is excellent for placing on your refrigerator or elsewhere that may keep it front of mind. It includes the attainment checklist for the unit as well as the foreign language vocabulary, memory statements, and literature selections that are recommended. As an alternative, in the shop (LifeAbundantlyBlog.com/Shop), you will find Memory Statement Cards for the memory statements to be displayed in a beautiful and convenient way in your home along with flashcards for your Spanish and/or French practice. We will discuss the foreign language and literature selections soon!

Activities + Field Trips + Explorations- In this section, for each unit, you will find activities, suggestions, and ideas to foster natural, gentle exploration of each unit's nature focus.

More Fun!
This section adds applicable songs, games, more traditional craft ideas for moms that like to include those, along with the important tools in the Term 1 Bundle from LifeAbundantlyBlog.com/shop that will be extremely helpful in teaching the material. You'll also find a page reference to the book Nature's Playground (look at Recommended Resources in the appendix for more information). The activities on the pages referenced may or may not directly relate to the Nature Focus of the unit, but they always include amazing, educational, and ingenious inspiration for spending time out of doors! This book is HIGHLY recommended!

What are the "attainments"?

What are these "attainments"? In a curriculum from the 1890's, Charlotte Mason outlined a list of "attainments" that she believed were **a challenging set of skills and knowledge that a well-educated child of 6 would do well to have.** In an excellent post from JuniperPines.com (http://bit.ly/AttainmentList), Marjorie clarifies misconceptions about this "Attainment List." The main take-away here is that this list of skills is not for a child to have mastered BY the age of 6, but rather to be challenged with AT the age of 6. What does this mean? It essentially means that the following list of attainments are not a "Kindergarten Readiness" list but instead would be considered Miss Mason's "Kindergarten" program.

So this begs the question: **should we be endeavoring to begin this list of attainments with our 4 and 5 year olds?** Will we keep them from their full potential by encumbering them with lessons? My answer to these questions is two-fold (and based on my own personal convictions and interpretations of research):

1. **Counter-culturally, I propose that we must not always approach everything in absolutes.** Yes, childhood is short and days can be busy. However, when our children are 3-5 years old, they are often awake for 12-14 hours each day. Is that not enough time to let them have an abundance of open-ended play both inside and out-of-doors as well as begin early, natural, developmentally appropriate instruction? For our family, we believe that 20 minutes of intentional instruction woven into the natural rhythm of our day beginning around age 2 or 3 will only give them an advantage, as long as they are not forcibly resistant to it.

2. **What do you think?** That is to say- as mentioned in the introduction- for your family, for your children, based on your home education goals, the hours in your day, and your impassioned prayer for God's guidance, do you believe that you ought to begin instruction with your child, given their age, temperament, maturity, and other life circumstances? This answer will inherently be very different for each mother AND each child. Once you are certain about your child's readiness, you can walk confidently forward in the way God is leading you.

For your convenience, the attainments are listed next, in their entirety, but are also included in the Term 1 Bundle as an attractive poster to display in your home. We will be tackling roughly half of these attainments, by-the-way, as we walk through all 3 terms of Gentle + Classical Nature. **The remaining attainments are woven naturally into the fibers of The Gentle + Classical Preschool Level 2** (for ages 4-7, releasing late summer 2019).

On page 27 of Part 1 of this book, we will approach each attainment individually, dive deeply into its purpose, and discuss our method of accomplishing each, relying heavily upon Miss Mason's words and guidance.

List of Attainments Issued by Charlotte Mason
(in brief)

A FORMIDABLE LIST OF ATTAINMENT FOR A CHILD OF SIX
(items in this font will be covered within the 3 terms of GCN)

1. **To recite, beautifully, six easy poems** and hymns.

2. To recite, perfectly and beautifully, a parable and a psalm.

3. To add and subtract numbers up to ten, with dominoes or counters.

4. To read — what and how much, will depend on what we are told of the child; children vary much in their power of reading.

5. To copy in print-hand from a book.

6. **To know the points of the compass with relation to their own home, where the sun rises and sets, and the way the wind blows.**

7. **To describe the boundaries of their own home.**

8. **To describe any lake, river, pond, island, &c, within easy reach.**

9. To tell quite accurately (however shortly) three stories from Bible history, three from early English, and three from early Roman history.

10. **To be able to describe three walks and three views.**

11. **To mount in a scrap book a dozen common wildflowers, with leaves (one every week); to name these, describe them in their own words, and say where they found them.**

12. **To do the same with the leaves and flowers of six forest trees.**

13. **To know six birds, by song, colour, and shape.**

14. **To send in certain Kindergarten or other handiwork, as directed.**

15. **To tell three stories about their own "pets" — rabbit, dog, or cat.**

16. **To name twenty common objects in French, and say a dozen little sentences.**

17. To sing one hymn, one French song, and one English song.

18. **To keep a caterpillar, and tell the life story of a butterfly from his own observations.**

We will dive fully into how GCN is designed to cover these attainments momentarily. For now, let's look at planning and scheduling information to keep our eyes on the "big picture."

Scheduling + Planning "Quick Start"

As detailed on page 11, Gentle + Classical Nature is a program that consists of 3 terms. Once all terms are released, you are free to choose which of the 3 you want to use and in what order. Keep in mind that the attainments are covered over the course of ALL 3 terms. However, if the attainments are not of importance to you and you are seeking to utilize the "nature focus" content alone, then you are fully free to choose the term that suits your preferences once they are all available. For review they are:

TERM 1: INLAND WATERWAYS AND FORESTS
TERM 2: COASTAL WOODLANDS AND OCEANS (releasing fall 2019)
TERM 3: DOWN ON THE FARM AND AROUND THE WORLD (releasing winter 2019)

Each term consists of 12 units that (aside from building and reviewing the attainments) are truly stand-alone. In all, there are 36 units in the full 3-term program.

You will need to make the following decisions and follow these steps during your planning phase. If you hope to get started implementing the program quickly, below are a set of details to cover before you dive in!

"Quick Start"

1. If you will be utilizing the attainment portion of the program, begin with term 1. (You'll want to work sequentially through all 3 terms.)
2. If the attainments are not important to you, select a term to begin with (once all are available).
3. If you will be pursuing the attainments, utilize the Attainment Planning Sheet (in the appendix) to select your Walk/View and "Body of Water" for study. (The section titled "Attainments: Detailed" on page 27 will help you here.)
4. Select the appropriate level for each of your children. (See page 25.)
5. If you have a child older than 7 who you want to integrate into this program, acquire the Upper Grammar Expansion Pack to include their Level 3 book lists, schedules, copywork, poetry, and more (available at LifeAbundantlyBlog.com/shop).
6. Now that you have chosen the term you will begin with, you know whether you will pursue the attainments or not, and you have chosen a level, you will want to consider whether you will complete a unit in one week or two. You will find detailed scheduling help and samples on pages 21-23.
7. Find and secure required books for the program. It's best to purchase the "spine" books if you are able and then place holds on any "menu" books specific to each unit at your local library. (You'll find more information about book selection on the next page.)

8. If you would like to utilize the life cycle worksheets, 3-Part Montessori Cards, poetry cards, Memory Statement cards, French and Spanish flashcards, and the Nature Collection Journal, head to LifeAbundantlyBlog.com/Shop and click "Materials for Gentle + Classical Nature Term 1."

Book Notes

Each section titled "Literature Selections" on the "Unit At-a-Glance" page in this curriculum indicates both a required reading (selected because of its beautiful language, imagery, literary significance, and ready availability) and a "menu" of additional reading options. The REQUIRED books are kept to a minimum and are also detailed on the "Highly Recommended Resources + Books" in the appendix.

Each level of the program has its own "book menu." These menus were carefully curated, but they are not exhaustive. There are many more fantastic books available that cover each of these subjects. You can find a convenient, printable version of all 12 "book menus" in the Term 1 Bundle.

Here are a few tips and some helpful information:
- Use what you have available in your home or at your local library. There are many excellent books not on my list!
- Don't stress about books. There are numerous great ones, and the important thing is to make reading aloud an integral part of your day from an early age.
- Avoid reading outside during free exploration time. Make sure you don't substitute one of these precious events for the other. I encourage you to make time for both.
- You might choose to read several books per unit or "row" one book multiples times over a unit. Both are great options!
- There are a couple of books that we rely on unit after unit (referred to as "spine" or "highly recommended" throughout the text). To keep costs low and to appeal to as many ages with as few books as possible, I chose books that can be read again and again with deeper and deeper understanding over several weeks, that are widely available for purchase or in your local library, and still have excellent illustrations and beautiful language.
- Each level has its own term read aloud option. I have a suggested pace of reading (outlined on each "Unit At-A-Glance" page) that allots to read the full chapter book over the 12 units. But again, this shouldn't be a huge stress point. Reading aloud is a great opportunity to train little ones in attentiveness and self-control. Keep it positive and within "fruitful frustration" for everyone involved. The pace that you keep isn't nearly as important as the experience!
- I bribe my toddlers with chocolate chips to listen to read alouds! They are much more attentive when they have a "high value" snack that comes along with listening. Do what works for you! We don't bribe them at any other time, but I find it helps make a positive association with something that can be quite challenging for them.
- If you are choosing a read aloud for multiple levels to be done at once (i.e. Morning Basket), I suggest that you go with the lower level read aloud. They are still excellent for upper grammar

children, but won't tire out your shorter listeners.

☐ The picture book series used as the "spine" through all 3 terms by Kate Messner are considered required reading. However- truly- if getting those is outside of your budget considerations, this program is overwhelmingly rich without them. You have several options for reading these: Read each book once during each unit or read them more frequently. Keep in mind that they are read again and again over several units as we learn new organisms and natural cycles, so pace yourself. I feel like once per unit is perfectly sufficient.

Sample Schedules (3 Day, 5 Day, 2 Week)

For your convenience, detailed schedules are available for Unit 1 on pages 49-51. Below you'll find a general suggested flow for each unit, with 3 different schedules.

3 Day Schedule

Day 1	Day 2	Day 3
Morning Basket: Include term reading, poem recitation, handicraft, and memory statement introduction	Morning Basket: Include term reading, poem recitation, handicraft, memory statement practice	Morning Basket: Include term reading, poem recitation, handicraft
Read science spine text (Messner) and discuss in relation to memory statement	Read additional read aloud from "book menu"	Read additional read aloud from "book menu"
Use foreign language terms during discussion and exploration, as appropriate	Begin chosen activity or unit project. Document if desired in Nature Diary (*separate from Nature Collection Journal; for child's own notes and drawings)	Visit your attainment for the unit (Walk/View or "Body of Water"), practicing observation and remembering skills, reflecting child's level
During outside explorations, be sure to collect the flower/tree parts for the unit (when applicable). Add to your Nature Collection Journal, Visit time and again to review and track seasonal changes (pages 30-34 for more tips!)	Use French/Spanish flashcards to learn and review terms.	Practice memory statement during discussions on walk
Begin any unit project or activity	Play "picture-painting" or other memory games today as a warm-up (page 29)	Complete any related activities or worksheets from the Bundle or other resources
	Use 3-Part Montessori Cards	
	Outside Exploration	

5 Day Schedule

Day 1

Morning Basket: Include term reading, poem recitation, handicraft, and memory statement introduction

During outside explorations, be sure to collect the flower/tree parts for the unit (when applicable). Add to <u>Nature Collection Journal</u>, (pages 30-34 for more tips!)

Use foreign language terms during discussion and exploration, as appropriate, reviewing old ones as well

Day 2

Morning Basket: Include term reading, poem recitation, handicraft, practice memory statement

Read Science spine text (Messner)

Begin chosen activity or unit project. Document if desired in Nature Diary

Play warm-up "picture-painting" or memory games (page 29)

Outside Exploration

Day 3

Morning Basket: Include term reading, poem recitation, handicraft

Visit your attainment for the unit (Walk/View or "Body of Water"), practicing observation and remembering skills, reflecting child's level (page 29)

Practice memory statement during discussions on walk

Use French/Spanish flashcards to practice new terms

Day 4

Morning Basket: Include term reading, poem recitation, handicraft, and memory statements

Read aloud additional book from "book menu"

Discuss reading and relationship to memory statement

Outside Exploration

Use foreign language terms during discussion and exploration, as appropriate

Day 5

Morning Basket: Include term reading, poem recitation, handicraft, practice memory statement

Finalize or continue working on project or a unit activity as needed

Review French/Spanish terms with flashcards again

Mentally "walk through" your Walk/View or "Body of Water" with your child from Day 3 (depending upon level)

©Gentle + Classical Nature

2 Week Schedule

Daily

Morning Basket: Include term reading, poem recitation, handicraft, and memory statement introduction/practice

Outside Exploration: As outlined on pages 30-34, spend as much time outside daily in free exploration and collecting/observing flowers, trees, birds.

Day 1

Read Science Spine (Messner)

Introduce new foreign language terms with flashcards (reviewing previously learned ones as well)

Day 2

Begin Chosen activity or unit project.

Read a unit-related book from "book menu"

Use foreign language terms while reading aloud when possible

Day 3

Play "picture-painting" or other memory games today as a warm-up (page 29)

Utilize any related activity sheet or printable you may have planned

Day 4

Visit the unit's attainment (Walk/View or "Body of Water"), practicing observation and remembering skills, reflecting child's level

Look for opportunities to drop "nature nuggets," utilize the memory statements, or practice foreign language terms

Day 5

Continue to work on unit project or do a second activity for unit

During outside explorations, be sure to collect the flower/tree parts for the unit (when applicable); add to Nature Collection Journal and revisit to review when possible

Day 6

Play a sorting or sequencing game with your 3-Part Montessori Cards from the Bundle

Review French or Spanish with flashcards

Day 7

Read a second unit-related book from "book menu"

Practice remembering all that you can from the attainment visit on Day 4 or play more "picture-painting"/memory games, based on level

Day 8

Finalize any projects from unit

Utilize any remaining unit-specific activity sheets

Consider having your child share all they've learned via an oral or written narration with another family member

Levels

Throughout the rest of this program, you will see "levels" referenced, especially in relation to memory statements and literature selections. We have 3 levels that I will refer to that are loosely based upon age. **What is more important than age, in regard to these levels, is the ability to attend, to memorize, and to understand the material.** As a rough guide, they are as follows:

Level 1: Ages 3-6; statements are very specific and brief; readings are much shorter and simplified
Level 2: Ages 5-9; statements are broader with more detail; readings are longer with more detail
Level 3: Ages 8-12; statements combine levels 1 and 2 or alternatives are offered that are much longer and more detailed; readings include much greater details and include multiple chapter books

You will notice an overlap in ages above. Since there is a huge range of abilities in reading, attention, and memorization that is all considered normal, I've been generous with the age ranges. In your own home, you'll likely see a distinct difference in abilities to listen to read alouds or focus on a handicraft among your own children, based more on nature than age. (Side Note: If attention is an issue in your home, I HIGHLY recommend that you read Volume 1: Home Education by Charlotte Mason!) What is easy to one 4-year-old to attend to or repeat might be quite challenging for an 8-year-old, while both are completely within "norm." Furthermore, with learning disabilities and other developmental variations in mind, these levels should be chosen based on skill and maturity rather than age.

IMPORTANT NOTE ABOUT LEVEL 3: While you will find the Level 3 Memory Statements included in Gentle + Classical Nature (and in the Term 1 Bundle), there is no further reference to Level 3 in this base program. If you would like to stretch the program to include all of your elementary students or want to customize it for an older child because you're just now learning about Charlotte Mason, a Upper Gramar Expansion Pack is available in the shop that includes age appropriate literature suggestions, poetry, activities and projects along with copywork and other upper elementary-related resources.

> **STOP:** It's not a bad idea to go ahead and prayerfully consider where each of your students fall in these levels. Browsing through the curriculum will also help you gain insight. There is no "WRONG" answer- only what works for your family. Seek what is a comfortable fit with very light stretching— what I refer to as "fruitful frustration." If in doubt, go with the lower level. It will be much easier (and more encouraging) to go up a level than have to move down one.

ATTAINMENTS

(IN DETAIL)

Let's now discuss the PROCESS that accomplishes these attainments in detail. In this section, we will review each individual attainment— in detail— and discuss what we will be doing to attain it, along with methods you will employ to help your child reap the most benefit from their work. We will rely heavily upon Miss Mason's own words as we dig deeper.

> **STOP**: Please don't be overwhelmed. If these methods of home education are new to you, it's easy to throw it to the side and assume you can't do it. The GOAL of GCN is to educate and equip you in all of YOUR goals. I encourage you to take this one piece, one step, one moment at a time. This guide is here for you to return to and reference again and again.

1. **To recite, beautifully, six easy poems** and hymns.

While we will not be practicing hymns as a goal of Gentle + Classical Nature, we will learn to beautifully recite poems. (During the 3 terms of GCN, we will schedule to recite 6 poems, with hymnal study being accomplished in Gentle + Classical Preschool Level 2.) As one might expect, the poetry we will select for use with GCN will be nature themed. This is absolutely not required and you may want to choose different poems, based on your child's reading level (or repeating level) that are not nature themed. The Term 1 Bundle houses a nice selection for Levels 1 and 2 along with gorgeous art related to each poem. We will plan to recite (unto eventual memorization) 3 poems over Term 1 of GCN. (Though if your child has a knack or significant aversion, please follow his lead.) The other 3 poems will be spaced over Terms 2 and 3.

As far as "beautifully recite", this is what Miss Mason has to say in reference to "The Children's Art" (or recitation): "The child should speak beautiful thoughts so beautifully, with such delicate rendering of each nuance of meaning, that he becomes to the listener the interpreter of the author's thought.... The child is led to find the just expression of the thought for himself; never is the poor teacher allowed to set a pattern– 'say this as I say it.' The ideas are kept well within the child's range, and the expression is his own... (Recitation) will behoove every educated man and woman to be able to speak effectively in public; and in learning to recite you learn to speak." (v1; p223-224)

Tips for recitation with pre-readers: We obviously begin memory work and recitation with pre-readers in this program. I've done this with all of my children and see great fruit in my teen daughters. A few quick suggestions:
　1. Keep your expectations realistic (attention and memory spans seem to vary by the day). We frequently have great "remembering" days followed by "complete blank" days.
　2. Record the recitation with your child so that they can use the video for independent practice. I record their face (which they enjoy to watch) and say a portion, having them repeat after me, just as we would do in person. They then watch and practice with the video each day. They enjoy it, AND it gives them independence.
　3. Have them share their recitation with family members as soon as they can.

---

2. To recite, perfectly and beautifully, a parable and a psalm.
3. To add and subtract numbers up to ten, with dominoes or counters.

4. To read — what and how much, will depend on what we are told of the child; children vary much in their power of reading.

5. To copy in print-hand from a book.

Attainments 2-5 will not be covered in GCN but will be naturally integrated into Gentle + Classical Preschool Level 2 (late summer 2019), however the Term 1 Bundle does include copywork of the Memory Statements for your convenience.

---

6. **To know the points of the compass with relation to their own home, where the sun rises and sets, and the way the wind blows.**

7. **To describe the boundaries of their own home.**

These attainments (6 & 7) will be covered in TERM 3: DOWN ON THE FARM AND AROUND THE WORLD. As such, they will be explained in detail in that term's introduction.

---

8. **To describe any lake, river, pond, island, within easy reach.** (Referred to as "Body of Water" in GCN.)

9. To tell quite accurately (however shortly) three stories from Bible history, three from early English, and three from early Roman history.

10. **To be able to describe three walks and three views.** (Referred to as a Walk/View throughout GCN.)

Required Reading for Mom: Volume 1: Home Education by Charlotte Mason, pages 48-49; "Picture-Painting."

STOP! This next section is SUPER helpful for developing these skills.

While attainment 9 will not be covered in GCN, attainments 8 and 10 will be alternated each unit and will guide our weekly nature explorations. We begin in Unit 1 with the first Walk/View and then alternate each unit, focusing back and forth between these two attainments. Each term will include absorbing the sights, sounds, and smells of one Walk/View and one "Body of Water." (There are examples and details in the appendix to help you choose a Walk/View and "Body of Water.")

Here is an example of how our viewing and reviewing will progress: In Unit 1, you will visit the Walk/View for Term 1 for the first time and learn how to observe and "picture-paint" what you see until it is firmly and permanently planted into their minds (over the course of all 12 units in the term). In Unit 2, you will visit the "Body of Water" you've chosen and do the same, while also discussing and remembering the Walk/View from Unit 1. In Unit 3, you return to your Walk/View and continue your progression of "picture-painting" the scene. Thusly you will alternate these two locations each week (or biweekly, based on your preferred schedule), until you and your child can hold a robust and detailed image in your mind of both locations (again, accomplished over the course of all 12 units in the term.).

One caution that Miss Mason gives is that while viewing is of little to no effort, **there is an inherent strain in articulating what they are seeing in their mind's eye.** "Picture-painting" is of great value but should be used judiciously. Employing this technique once on the walk then once later in the week to review is more than enough.

"Picture-Painting" + Memory Games + Tips

1. **Follow your child's lead.** Your child might be able to listen to a read aloud for 30 minutes but still not be able to articulate the images and details he is seeing in his mind or with his eyes. The skill of putting WORDS to what we are seeing, hearing, and experiencing is truly a challenging skill. Baby steps, baby steps. Meet your child right where he is and keep the process light and fun!

2. **For Level 1 students, consider having them share observations while keeping their eyes open, as a stepping stone.** Verbalizing what they're seeing with their eyes open has to come before verbalizing mental images and is a definite, separate skill. You may also share (aloud) your own observations to demonstrate the process of seeing and sharing with them. Modeling is a powerful tool!

3. **Model what this looks like to your child, as often as comes naturally.** Make it your own habit to practice "picture-painting" and share those "images" with your children. This doesn't have to be something that's formal, prepared, or grand. Sharing your descriptions of the characteristics of rocks, trees, paintings, or any other object you're both looking at will do the trick.

"Look at this beautiful rock. It's about the size of my fist and is very cold. I love how the bottom is damp and muddy and the top is dimpled. Do you see that fuzzy stuff that's green? That's moss growing on the rock." Later that evening say, "Do you remember that rock we looked at today? What do you remember about it?" Follow their lead. If they can't come up with much, close your eyes and share your own remembrance, painting a picture for them by being as descriptive as possible. Help them to experience what it's like to SEE in their mind from the words someone else is using. Their personal experience with "seeing" something in their imagination from your vivid description will help make a distinct connection with the importance of this skill.

4. **For youngest children who are overwhelmed at the idea of describing an entire view or pond, play brief, warm-up, "picture-painting" games.** Any game that relies on your child's visual memory will build this "muscle." Basic card matching games are an excellent example. You can also utilize the 3-Part Montessori Cards by making two copies and laying them face down. Once your child is capable of successfully playing matching games with a dozen or so cards, then try small "picture-painting" challenges with various, simple objects.

Example: Lay 3 rocks on the ground, all distinctly different in size and shape. Ask your child to observe them with their eyes open and share as many physical, descriptive details as possible. If he doesn't grasp the concept, give him an example: "I see 3 rocks. One is very large and black. The one below it is smooth and white. The last one below that is red and bumpy and small." Once you've demonstrated this, encourage your child to try their hand at it. You can add more rocks and graduate to looking and describing with their eyes closed once they understand how to use describe verbally. Try these small "memory muscle-building" games whenever your child seems receptive, in different settings, and using various objects.

5. **Progress slowly.** As they get better at these games over time, encourage more detail, more objects, and longer spans of attention— very, very gradually, following their natural growth in these skills. Only once they can play these games successfully with several objects, a tree, or a small garden, should you challenge them with a Walk/View or a "Body of Water." Your wise building of these skills will make their eventual progress into these two attainments all the more pleasurable and memorable for you both.

> **STOP:** With this in mind, this portion of the attainments (remembering an entire Walk/View or "Body of Water") maybe be suitable for your Level 2 students and older. However, don't allow this to stop you from playing these developmentally appropriate and powerful games with your Level 1 students. You can always have them cycle back through the GCN attainments when they are ready.

6. **Keep in mind, that for younger children, this could be a skill that you need to build <u>over years</u>.** These attainments are for a child "of 6" and are considered formidable. Don't get discouraged! Think of the gift your persistent gentleness is for your child's mental and character development. For children under 6, you are doing just as much good playing memory and "picture-painting" games as you would be helping them to observe and remember a Walk/View because you are meeting them where they are. It's all a beautiful, gentle process!

> **STOP**: After you have read the assigned reading in <u>Volume 1: Home Education</u> (related to "picture-painting"), flip to the Attainment Planning and Tracking sheet in the appendix. You will use this goal setting sheet and tracker for all 3 Terms. Go ahead and choose (at minimum) the first Walk/View and first "Body of Water" you will be visiting and observing. **Keep a few things in mind:** Ideally, you need to visit one or the other each week (or biweekly if you do a unit over 2 weeks), so you want them to be rather convenient. They do not have to be grand! If your resources are limited, choose from what's available. If you don't have a "Body of Water" available, then skip it. It's seriously not a huge deal! You could even substitute a local building or landmark of importance or a singular tree. This is a FORMIDABLE list and is a great goal, but it should not be a point of worry, stress, perfection, or comparison. See page 113 for more considerations.

---

11. **To mount in a scrap book a dozen common wildflowers, with leaves (one every week); to name these, describe them in their own words, and say where they found them.**

In this attainment, we are fortunate to simply be able to follow Miss Mason's specific instructions: "every wild flower that grows in their neighborhood, they should know quite well; should be able to describe the leaf- its shape, size growing from the root or from the stem; the manner of flower- a head of flowers, a single flower; a spike, etc. And having made the acquaintance of a wild flower, so that they can never forget it or mistake it, they should examine the spot where they find it, so that they will know for the future in what sort of ground to look for such and such a flower... To make collections of wildflowers for several months, press them, and mount them neatly on squares of cartridge paper; with the English name, habitat, and date of finding each, afford much happy occupation and, at the same time, much useful training; better still is it to accustom children to make careful brushdrawings of the flowers that interest them, of the whole plant where possible." (v1; p51-42)

The extent to which your child is able to observe and record his collections will be very much influenced by his age and maturity. However, don't allow the age of a younger child to stop the process of observing and collecting. In our home (due to little perfectionists), we stick to collection before the age 5, for the most part. Then, as they grow in greater dexterity and in fine motor skills, we begin brushdrawing and sketching.

In this program of study, we will alternate weeks between collecting and observing wildflowers, trees (attainment 12), and birds (attainment 13). Each week, you will also be reminded to review the previous weeks' observations and collections. The Attainment Planner and Tracking sheet in the appendix (and an additional progress tracker in the Term 1 Bundle) will be very helpful in keeping up with what you've learned and need to review.

KEY NOTE: While this curriculum has a general progress of one new observation (of various kind) each unit, the PACE is not of the utmost importance. Some children are naturally born with an eye for observing details and articulating their thoughts. It will come naturally to some and need to be trained and demonstrated time and again for others. One child of 3 may be able to distinguish between two similar birds in just a week of study while a six year old struggles to see the difference between a long leaf pine and an oak tree. Please don't be discouraged and get hung up on ages and attainments. Your patience in this allows for their true education to take place— creating new connections and building new skills. **Allow this process of collecting and remembering to take as long as it takes.** You can always use the Planning and Tracking Sheet in the appendix at your own pace, not the pace set forth in the unit.

Our family's general technique for nature study and nature collection is detailed below. Keep in mind, this is what works for my family, based upon our ages, lifestyle, and preferences. Each mother has to decide for herself what this looks like for her family.

- 🌲 Depending upon the weather, we either head out first thing in the morning or in the early afternoon. We try very hard not to allow the weather to dissuade us, and my goal is to be out of doors as much as possible. That said, I don't have the staff at my home that some early Charlotte Mason educators may have had! Therefore, we do as much as possible, without any guilt for not hitting the lofty goal of 5-6 hours each day.
- 🌲 We were recently blessed to move to a 10 acre property, which I realize is not the case for everyone. However, having lived in the suburbs for several years, we essentially maintained the same schedule, with a narrower area to wonder. (I encourage you to read Volume 1: Home Education, pages 43-44 if you're feeling discouraged about the availability of out-of-doors time and space in your

schedule or location.)

🌲 On average, we spend 2 hours outside each day. On particularly delightful days this might be 5+ hours. In horrible weather, it may be 0-30 minutes.

🌲 We do not take our nature journals with us. We simply gather everything that catches our eye while we are out. I may steer them toward a particular flower or plant I would like for us to learn about. They gather all of their treasures, and we pile them onto our nature collection table.

🌲 Later in the day, when the opportunity presents itself, we then choose our flower (or tree) of focus and attach its various parts into our Nature Collection Journal. My older girls join us a few days a week. They collect and press but also use watercolors, charcoals, or sketch their finds (whichever appeals to them). My daughters (middle and high school), spend time with the extension page in our Nature Collection Journals (LifeAbundantlyBlog.com/shop), identifying the genus and species and being more specific about various attributes of the plant and its habitat. We choose to use watercolor paper and paste/tape it into the journal to avoid upset feelings if an illustration doesn't turn out like someone hoped the first time.

🌲 The Nature Collection Journal was created to use in tandem with Gentle + Classical Nature. It has space for 12 wildflowers, 6 trees, and 6 other nature observations and collections (like birds, shells, rocks, and more). In the Appendix of the Nature Collection Journal, I provide charts for identifying leaf structures and arrangements along with advanced pages for middle school and high school students.

🌲 Once I've determined a particular tree or flower that we will seek to learn by heart, I make sure that each day we visit that tree. I'll ask if anyone remembers the name, allowing my youngest to go first. If they don't know, I simply remind them, mention a few details that I can observe about its leaves, bark, fruit, nuts, or flower, (thusly modeling observations for them) and then move along. Each day that we pass by, we basically repeat the process. I ask if they remember, we share observations about the specimen, and keep going.

🌲 In this way, we are consistently reviewing the same specimen but in an extremely casual way. This also highlights an important point (that Miss Mason mentioned as well): The trees/plants that you choose to commit to heart should be "in their neighborhood" so that you can easily visit, discuss, observe, and review without fuss or much travel.

🌲 With your youngest learners (those under 6), I encourage you to keep this super casual and fun! Of course, we want it to be fun for all ages, but if our 4 year old is resistant to answering our questions or generally showing no interest at all, we don't want to begin a power struggle over naming the white ash. This is likely not a hill to die on with a strong-willed toddler!

🌲 An important note from Miss Mason on leaving our children alone to observe vs teaching them: "Of the evils of modern education, few are worse than this— that the perpetual cackle of his elders leaves the poor child not a moment of time, or an inch of space, wherein to wonder— and grow. At the same time, here is the mother's opportunity to train the seeing eye, the hearing ear, and to drop seeds of truth into the open soul of the child, which shall germinate, blossom, and bear fruit, without further help or knowledge of hers (the mother's)." (v1; p44)

🌲 As you can see from the quote above, much time should be allowed for free play and exploration. However, that is not at the sacrifice of using opportunities for learning, throughout your day. The art of educating is being prepared ahead and having a keen instinct for when to add bits of knowledge and when to leave your child alone. **Nature Nuggets, included in each unit, will equip you to do just this!**

---

12. **To do the same with the leaves and flowers of six forest trees.**

We are fortunate again to have Miss Mason's direct thoughts and instruction in our observation and collection of trees: "Children should be made early intimate with the trees, too; should pick out half a dozen trees, oak, elm, ash, beech, in their winter nakedness, and take these to be their year-long friends... They may wait to learn the names of the trees until the leaves come... They (the children) have the delight of discovering that the great trees have flowers, too, flowers very often of the same hue as their leaves, and that some trees put off having their leaves until their flowers have come and gone. By-and-by there is the fruit, and the discovery that every tree with exceptions which they need not learn yet- and every plant bears fruit, 'fruit and seed after his kind.' All this is stale knowledge to older people, but one of the secrets of the educator is to present nothing as stale knowledge, but to put himself in the position of the child, and wonder and admire with him; for every common miracle which the child sees with his own eyes makes of him for the moment another Newton." (v1; p 52-54 partial)

Here are some important ideas to note:

🌳 While Miss Mason suggests we begin our study of trees in the winter, there really is no time like the present. You need not wait until the winter to begin.

🌳 The procedure set forth in GCN is that we will take one specific tree under our observation for 2 units, but we will continuously review those we previously visited.

🌳 Over all 3 Terms, we will have made close acquaintance with a half dozen and observed them all (in review and in relationship) throughout that time.

🌳 Just like with wildflowers, you can collect, brushdraw, sketch, etc. The Nature Collection Journal (LifeAbundantlyBlog.com/Shop) has space to collect and record observations for children 3 through high school and was created just for this purpose.

🌳 For our youngest students (in the Nature Collection Journal), you can help them mount their findings and use the journal to review when time doesn't allow a visit to the tree. You can record for them and use the provided prompts (in the Nature Collection Journal) to help your child develop an eye and vocabulary for describing various aspects of the bark, roots, leaves, or fruit.

🌳 For Level 2 students, you can add an additional step of sketching, watercolor, or brushdrawing. We prefer to do so on separate paper and attach it into the Journal (to avoid mistakes that are discouraging).

🌳 For Level 3 students, in the Appendix of the Nature Collection Journal, you will find an expansion form for detailing important information about the tree's habitat, leaf arrangement and formation, and various other important scientific facts about the species you are studying. Using this page ensures that this program is more than sufficient for a middle school student's botany study. Posters are also available in the appendix of the Nature Collection Journal to help identify those aspects as well.

🌳 Charlotte Mason on nature diaries and brushdrawing: "As soon as he is able to keep it himself, a nature-diary is a source of delight to a child... While he is quite young (five or six), he should begin to illustrate his notes freely with brushdrawings; he should have a little help at first in mixing colors, in the way of principles, not directions... As for drawing, instruction no doubt has its time and place; but his nature-diary should be left to his own initiative. A child of six will produce a dandelion, poppy, daisy, iris with its leaves, impelled by the desire to represent what he sees, with surprising vigor and correctness." (v1; p54-55)

As you can see, our <u>Nature Collection Journal</u> varies from Miss Mason's directions for a "nature diary." As such, for Level 2 children and older, you might consider allowing them a completely separate notebook just for collecting and recording anything they might like. However, there are additional "nature find" pages in the Nature Collection Journal for finds outside of the specific trees and wildflowers we are studying in GCN. This is totally up to you, Mama!

---

13. **To know six birds, by song, colour, and shape.**

In this attainment, during the weeks we aren't collecting wildflowers or tree parts, we will be observing and recording birds to commit to heart so that we can know their species based upon their song alone.

There is a particular skill that Miss Mason discusses in volume 1 called "sight-seeing." I believe that bird observation and study is a fantastic opportunity to employ this method of developing a keen eye for observing and committing details to memory. It's viewed as a game, slightly different than "picture-painting," but with very similar outcomes and skills employed.

Here's how she describes it: "while whits are fresh and eyes are keen, she (mother) sends them off on an exploring expedition— Who can see the most and tell the most, about yonder hillcock or brook, hedge or copse. This is an exercise that delights children and may be endlessly varied, carried on in the spirit of a game, and yet with the exactness and carefulness of a lesson. 'Find out all that you can about that cottage at the foot of the hill; but do not pry about too much.' Soon they are back, and there is a crowd of excited faces, and a hubbub of tongues, and random observations are shot breathlessly into mother's ear.... This is all play to the children, but the mother is doing invaluable work; she is training their powers of observation and expression, increasing their vocabulary and their range of ideas by giving them the name and the uses of an object at the right moment... And she is training her children in truthful habits, but making them careful to see the fact and to state it exactly, without omission or exaggeration." (v1; p46-47)

I highly encourage you to read the full section in the original volume as she gives an excellent (lengthy) example of what this exchange might look like. One "variation" would be to do the same with a bird that has caught your eye. Have your child go across the meadow or park to sneak as closely to their chosen target as possible (equipping them with binoculars if possible). Have them work to articulate as many observations as they can upon returning to you. Just like with "picture-painting," you will likely need to extract some answers and give numerous examples yourself. This is simply another way to make the process of observing, remembering, and sharing into a fun, educational game that children delight in to repeat time and again!

Your bird observations can also be recorded in your <u>Nature Collection Journal</u> as well. There are a variety of apps available for identifying birds and their calls. We really like www.AllAboutBirds.org and use it (and YouTube) regularly. Bird observation is discussed further in Unit 7.

---

14. **To send in certain Kindergarten or other handiwork, as directed.**

Handicrafts are incredibly beneficial in a number of ways, especially in the development of fine motor skills and hand-eye coordination. Our goal in GCN for handicrafts, if you choose to implement them, is that you would select one handicraft per term. I have included an entire "menu" of handicrafts in the Term 1 Bundle, and I've highlighted the crafts that are inherently nature-related.

You'll see in the appendix, on the Attainment Selection and Tracking sheet, that there is an area for you to record your choice of handicraft. While we schedule one per term, you are free to skip this all together or try something new each week. An excellent source of nature-related, beautifully planned handicrafts is a product called Rooted Childhood at RootedChildhood.com

Here's what Miss Mason has to say about handicrafts: "they (children) should not be employed in making futilities such as pea and stick works, paper mats, and the like." (v1; p315) I wholeheartedly agree, but there's also nothing wrong with an occasional paper craft either.

---

15. **To tell three stories about their own "pets" — rabbit, dog, or cat.**

While not every family has a pet, you might consider either getting one (very small) or "borrowing" one from a friend. Pet-sitting or visiting someone's pet would give your child the opportunity to have experiences that he could later relate to family and friends. This relating is the beginning groundwork for narration in the older years.

Whether it be pet stories or images they've painted upon the canvas of their minds, we are enabling our children to "carry it away with her, her own forever, a picture (or story) 'on view' just when she wants it." (v1; p50)

---

16. **To name twenty common objects in French, and say a dozen little sentences.**

In GCN, you will see a small menu of both French and Spanish vocabulary words each unit, and later in Term 3, short phrases. Charlotte Mason frequently spoke of learning French early, as French would have been the language of one of England's closest neighbors. However, those of us in the US may feel like Spanish would be of greater benefit for our children.

The language that you choose to practice with your child is completely up to you. There is no wrong answer. You also have the freedom to choose both or neither. In the attainments, Miss Mason outlines a "goal" of twenty objects and a half dozen little sentences. As such, that number is the hallmark for this program. Feel free to use this as a launchpad to add additional object names or to choose differently all together. Each noun chosen in this guide was selected based upon the terms in each unit's Memory Statement.

Here is (at-length) what Miss Mason has to say on the subject for children 6 and under in Volume 1: "The daily French lesson is that which should not be omitted. That children should learn French orally, <u>by listening to and repeating French words and phrases</u>; that they should begin so young that the difference of accent does not strike them, but they repeat the new French word all the same as if it were English and use it as freely; that they should learn a few- two or three, five or six- new French words daily, and that, at the same time, the old words should be kept in use- are points to be considered more fully hereafter: in the meantime, it is so important to keep tongue and ear familiar with French vocables, <u>that not a lesson should be omitted.</u> The French lesson may, however, be made to fit with the spirit of the other out-of-door occupations; the half-dozen words may be the parts- leaves, branches, bark, trunk of a tree, or colours of the flowers, or the movements of bird, cloud, lamb, child; in fact, the new French words should be but another form of expression for the ideas that for the time fill the child's mind." (v1; p80-81)

Here are two important points I want us to keep in mind:
1. Especially in children under the age of 6, all language should be transferred orally. What if you don't know French or Spanish? There are so many tools available at your disposal— Google translate, Duolingo, and great books from Usborne listed in book recommendations. You don't have to be fluent. You'll be learning alongside your child, utilizing internet resources to get the pronunciation correct, then planting those terms into your little one's mind, by-the-way. Don't be intimidated by foreign languages!

2. Miss Mason specifies that "not a lesson should be omitted." That is, of course, her opinion. As a mom of 4 homeschooled children, I can comfortably encourage you that you will likely miss a lesson, and that there is absolutely nothing wrong with that. Of course, if we believe that God has placed this curriculum in our path as a tool in educating our children, we should implement it with diligence, but never forget grace. I'm not a fan of absolutes as scripture says, "today or tomorrow we will go to this or that city, spend a year there...Why, you do not even know what will happen tomorrow." (James 4:13-14 partial). So let's always hold these ideals dearly but loosely, as we are "just a vapor."

18. **To keep a caterpillar, and tell the life story of a butterfly from his own observations.**

Each term of GCN will include a minimum of one "term project." There will be opportunities for more than this each term. It is up to you, of course, which and how many you choose to implement. The metamorphosis of a caterpillar (or tadpole) or the observation of an ant community hard at work creates a storehouse of experiences from which our children will draw from their entire lives. "Nature teaches us so gently, so gradually, so persistently, that he is never overdone, but goes on gathering little stores of knowledge about whatever comes before him." (v1; p67)

The importance of this gentle, slow process of observing nature as it transforms in front of him can

not be understated. "We older people... get most knowledge through words. We set the child to learn in the same way and find him dull and slow. Why? Because it is only with a few words in common use that he associates a definite meaning; all the rest are no more to him than the vocables of a foreign tongue. But set him face to face with a thing, and he is twenty times as quick as you are in knowing all about it." (v1; p67) The experience of watching metamorphosis is mind-blowing to even my dulled, mature mind. How much more to our children when introduced to it firsthand!

Here is what Miss Mason has to say about watching and recording observations:
"Children should be encouraged to watch, patiently and quietly, until they learn something of the habits and history of the bee, ant, wasp, spider, hairy caterpillar, dragon-fly, and whatever of larger growth comes in their way. (She then goes on, in detail, about building an ant farm, which we will utilize in Term 3.) The child who spends an hour in watching the ways of some new 'grub' he has come upon will be a man of mark yet. Let all he finds out about it be entered into his diary- by his mother, if writing be a labor for him. - where he finds it, what it is doing, or seems to him to be doing; its colour, shape, legs: some day he will come across the name of the creature, and will recognise the description of an old friend." (v1; p58)

Purpose + Importance of Memorization

As I've learned more about the roots of classical education, it seems me that there is some distortion of what a classical education is meant to be, with a frequent overzealous focus on memorization. Memorization is an excellent tool. I've seen the seeds that have been planted early on be put to great use in the older years myself. Our memorization here is just for that purpose- **to place pegs into little minds upon which terminology and exciting information can be hung upon for years to come.**

However, memorization in itself is NOT the end purpose. It is one tool of many in a gentle, classical education.

"Classical education is the inculcation of wisdom and virtue through a facility with the liberal arts and a familiarity with the Great Books. St. Thomas Aquinas defines wisdom as 'ordering things rightly.' If we grant this, then the relation between Sayers' trivium and classical education as it has always been conceived comes into better focus.

Process and content are not mutually exclusive. What is needed is a proper balance between the two, but a balance that places an unambiguous emphasis on the content that forms the student's soul. We cannot exclude method altogether—that would not be wise. **But neither can we exalt the process of education above its purpose.**" --Martin Cothran via MemoriaPress.com

Taking this into consideration, we can better understand that the trivium itself (and memorization) is a TOOL for which we can inspire wisdom and wonder in the minds of our children. The goal is not to create little poll-parrots (though they're very good at being such!) but rather to sow the fertile soil of their minds with seeds that will produce a bountiful harvest of knowledge and Godly wisdom.

Now that we have the importance of memorization in right perspective, let's consider our little "poll-parrots" for just a moment. Have you ever noticed how your toddler literally repeats everything you say? How they remember insane things you would have never anticipated them to recall? That as they grow older, though they don't "parrot" us the same, they still retain so much new information with only one or two exposures? They have amazing minds that are RIPE for planting seeds of knowledge that, over time, will develop into understanding and ultimately into application. (These 3 stages of development are referred to as the grammar, dialectic, and rhetoric stages in classical education.) **The end purpose of memorization is that our children would come out of their grammar education fully equipped with a vast storehouse of knowledge that they will build upon in the dialectic and rhetoric stages.**

It is with this in mind, that we begin early and frequent use of memorization in our homeschool. The implementation of memory work encompasses many habits like attention, responsiveness, perseverance, and obedience. In order to memorize, our children have to exercise their muscles of self-control, attend to what is being said, and repeat it back accurately (time and again). Despite my personal belief in its incredible importance in early education and its insurmountable value as your child progresses through the stages of education, it is not the ONLY aspect of classical education included in curriculum from Life, Abundantly. There are several other important, time-tested tools that are utilized as well to present the whole feast to our children.

What tools do we use in order to conduct a gentle, classical preschool in our homes?

Pretend play
Nature study
Hands-on interaction
Song and dance

Excellent literature
Narration
Memorization

Using a variety of approaches in teaching our children ensures that we are meeting them where they are, while appealing to their personal learning style and keeping much-needed variety in their school day.

In GCN, we focus on memorization, living books, narration, hands-on interaction, and nature study in order to introduce our children to our Creator's world. In Gentle + Classical Preschool, we also incorporate pretend play and song and dance into our days. Taken as a whole, the two programs work in tandem to bring the best aspects of classical education and the Charlotte Mason philosophy to our grammar-aged children.

Considering this information about memorization, in light of the attainments we've been focusing on, when and how does memorization come into play during our day?

Naturally. As mentioned earlier in regards to using "nature nuggets" to drop "seeds of truth into a child's soul," the memory statements can be introduced and included the same way. Alternatively, they can be practiced and recited during a specific "memory work" time in your day. In the suggested schedules, you'll see it is included during a "morning basket" time.

Over time, we have found it most effective to intentionally introduce the Memory Statements during a "memory work" time each day. We gather around our Memory Work Board and review each subject, singing or chanting each 2-3 times. Then, as we progress through our day, go on nature walks, or encounter something that brings it to mind, I will form a question and work with my little one to help them connect our memory statement to this story or experience in front of us. The goal is that this process of reviewing and integrating it into the day would be very "by-the-way" rather than overtly forced into situations in which your child is not engaged or receptive.

Memorization can work in your homeschool to support your other efforts in helping your children develop a firm foundation of knowledge that will serve them over the years. Most children enjoy this time and see it as a fun way to learn, especially when songs or chants are employed! With Level 1 children, I will continue to encourage you to keep it light and casual, building positive experience around memorization practice.

Each "Unit At-A-Glance" page includes the 3 levels of Memory Statements along with foreign language terms so that you will equipped with helpful information to sow new knowledge and terminology into growing, absorbent minds.

Alignment with The Gentle + Classical Preschool

If you are utilizing **The Gentle + Classical Preschool Level 1** (TGCP) alongside GCN, you'll find that many memory statements in GCN mirror the science portion of TGCP Level 1 but may include additional information and are not in the same order.

My suggestion, when using both curricula, is to skip the science statements in TGCP and simply utilize GCN in full (however many terms you would like). However, you might adopt the shorter versions from TGCP Level 1, where available.

Example:
In TGCP Level 1, Unit 1 Science is: Tadpoles turn into frogs.
In GCN, Unit 1: Tadpoles turn into froglets then into frogs.

GCN includes an additional piece of information as its age focus is 4+ rather than 2+. Use your own discernment and your child's aptitude for memorization when choosing which to utilize.

Gentle + Classical Nature replaces the science portion of **The Gentle + Classical Preschool Level 2** since the age focus is the same and they are created to be complementary. Furthermore, TGCP Level 2 will complete the "Formidable Attainments" set forth in this volume as well. Together, they are a beautiful and thorough early education (though you will still need your own phonics program and complete math program, based on when you choose to begin those). **While they are highly complementary, it is not required that you utilize both or begin them at the same time.** Over the span of time, they work exactly the same way- to help you child reach all of the attainments (and much more) in a gentle, classical way.

"The educational error of our day is that we believe too much in mediators. Now, Nature is her own mediator, undertakes, herself, to find work for eyes and ears, taste and touch; she will prick the brain with problems and the heart with feelings; and the part of the mother or teacher in the early years is to sow opportunities, and then to keep in the background, ready with a guiding or restraining hand only when these are badly wanted." (v1; p192-193)

Part 2

UNIT 1: AMPHIBIANS

OVERVIEW

In Unit 1, we launch our exploration into God's creation by exploring the amazing world of amphibians. Beyond our exploration of amphibians, we will begin our steady, slow immersion into the first attainments, our first term project, and the reading of nature-enriched literature!

Before we begin this lofty expedition into new and exciting territory, I have a word of encouragement for you from Charlotte Mason herself:

> "Self-education is the only possible education; the rest is mere veneer laid on the surface of a child's nature."

Let this thought bury itself warmly into the tenderest parts of your soul, creating roots and branching out, ready to overcome every worry, every fear, every fleeting moment of comparison as you dive headlong into a new season of home education. Our children are not blank slates, ready for our painting and covering and refinishing. If they were such, the education that we give them would lay only on the surface. No. They are whole persons, intricately and perfectly made in the image of their Creator, endowed with a thirst for his presence which is found so richly in his creation. Present the broad feast diligently. Partake in this education for yourself. Watch the beauty of this study create attachments, connections, and a living education inside of your child that will cultivate a harvest that lasts a lifetime.

NATURE NUGGETS

*Don't forget that ALL included links can be found at www.GentleClassical.com (black box labeled "Nature Nugget Links").
https://www.ducksters.com/animals/amphibians.php
https://kids.nationalgeographic.com/animals/hubs/amphibians/

TEACHER NOTES

It would be best to order or plan your tadpole project in advance, if possible, so that you can launch into it this week. Amazon typically stocks a variety of tadpole-to-frog life cycle kits.

If you are a little reticent about taking on a living pet, an alternative idea would be to find a local ditch, pond, or mud puddle that doesn't drain and visit it over the course of several weeks to watch the frogs' development in their natural habitat. In the northern hemisphere, frogspawn can typically be found in March/April. The tadpoles will hatch and begin their metamorphosis throughout the summer into the early fall. Fish eat tadpoles and frogspawn, so your best bet is a body of water that doesn't have fish, like shallow creeks or ditches that never drain.

If all else fails, utilizing this life cycle from Safari LTD makes a great replacement. It's available on Amazon and is called Life Cycle of a Frog.

I also encourage you to look on YouTube for videos. If you search "life cycle of a frog", the first several videos are fantastic!

This link has some great info about finding tadpoles, keeping them, and any potential licensing needed in certain states: http://bit.ly/tadpoles1

If you don't mind taking on a small pet, you don't have to limit yourselves to frogs. Newts and salamanders are also great pets. If you are considering a long-term amphibian pet, I encourage research. This link has many other resources available (http://bit.ly/Amph4Pets). Amphibians can live 5-10 years, carry disease, and can't be released into the wild when purchased from a pet store. This would be best for a Level 3 child.

UNIT 1 ATTAINMENTS

LOOKING FORWARD

As previously mentioned, in each of the 3 terms of Gentle + Classical Nature, we will slowly progress toward accomplishing many of Charlotte Mason's Formidable List of Attainments for a Child of 6. The remaining attainments are fleshed out and integrated into The Gentle + Classical Preschool Level 2 (while groundwork is laid in Level 1).

Before you began Unit 1, it was encouraged that you choose the following to focus on during Term 1 (the first 12 weeks of the program):

1 Walk/View
1 Poem
1 Handicraft
1 "Body of Water"
4 Wildflowers
2 Trees
2 Birds

If you have not done so, please refer back to page 27 to review the detailed notes about the attainments and make your choices for each area.

For Unit 1, you will be visiting your Walk/View for Term 1 for the first time. Please look in the appendix for information about identifying a Walk/View. You will visit this Walk/View every other unit for the entire term, so be sure that it is convenient to your home.

In the appendix, you will also find the Attainment Planning and Tracking sheet. Here you can write down your choices for each area we are focusing on. The Term 1 Bundle includes a selection of poetry, handicrafts, and an additional Attainment Progress Sheet that you'll find helpful. This certainly isn't required, but it is available if it is your preference to keep track of your child's progress through the school year. (I will add that this can be helpful in challenging seasons of homeschooling as well- to see how far you've come.)

Unit 1 Attainment Goals
- [ ] Identify and Visit Walk/View for Term 1
- [ ] "Picture-paint" with your child some portion of this Walk/View (see page 29)
- [ ] Begin Term Project #1 (weeks 1-6): Tadpole Metamorphosis
- [ ] Begin daily recitation of your first chosen nature poem
- [ ] Begin daily practice of chosen handicraft

UNIT 1 AT-A-GLANCE

Unit 1 Attainment Goals
- ☐ Identify and Visit Walk/View for Term 1
- ☐ "Picture-paint" with your child some portion of this Walk/View (see page 29)
- ☐ Begin Term Project #1 (weeks 1-6): Tadpole Metamorphosis
- ☐ Begin daily recitation of your first chosen nature poem
- ☐ Begin daily practice of chosen handicraft

FOREIGN LANGUAGE

SPANISH	FRENCH
frog- la rana	frog- la grenouille
pond- el estanque	pond- la mare
green- verde	green- vert

MEMORY STATEMENTS

LEVEL 1	LEVEL 2	LEVEL 3
Tadpoles turn into froglets then into frogs.	Frogs, toads, newts, and salamanders are amphibians.	Combine Level 1 & 2 OR: Amphibians breathe and absorb water through their skin. Some types of amphibians are frogs, toads, newts, and salamanders.

LITERATURE SELECTIONS

LEVEL 1
Term Reading 1: <u>Frog and Toad Storybook Treasury</u> (Lobel)- 22 pgs/unit over 12 units

Highly Recommended:
<u>Over and Under the Pond</u> (Messner)
<u>Nature Anatomy</u> (Rothman) (p194-195)

Optional Book Menu:
<u>Growing Frogs</u> (French)
<u>DK Encyclopedia of Animals</u> (p181-182)
<u>Mixed-Up Chameleon</u> (Carle)
<u>It's Mine</u> (Lionni)
<u>In the Small, Small Pond</u> (Fleming) *super short
<u>Pond Circle</u> (Franco)

LEVEL 2
Term 1 Reading: <u>Among the Pond People</u> (Pierson)- 16 Pages per unit

Highly Recommended:
Same as Level 1 Reading

Optional Book Menu:
<u>One Small Square: Pond</u> (Silver)
<u>From Tadpole to Frog</u> (Pfeffer)
<u>Mother West Wind "Where"</u> (Chapter 1) (Burgess)
<u>Frogs</u> (Gibbons)
<u>A Salamander's Life</u> (Himmelman)

ACTIVITIES + FIELD TRIPS + EXPLORATIONS

KEYS TO REMEMBER

- Except in the most dire weather, children should spend as much time outside as time allows.
- Invest in the best rain and cold weather gear possible.
- Nature exploration time is to be child-led with "key points" sown by Mom when the opportunity arises.

AMPHIBIAN EXPLORATIONS

- Search for puddles, creeks, and streams in which tadpoles might be developing.
- Look under rocks and old logs for salamanders and newts.
- Refer to your local/state wildlife departments (or Department of Conservation) for the best areas and times to locate various amphibians.
- Does your zoo have a special habitat for amphibians and reptiles?
- Does your local aquarium have amphibians on display? How about a natural history museum in your area?
- Here is a list of natural history museums in the US that may have herpetology exhibits: http://bit.ly/NatMusUS
- Visit the local pet store for no-commitment observation.

EVEN MORE FUN!

Song: 5 Green and Speckled Frogs

Activities: from Gentle + Classical Nature Term 1 Bundle
- 3-Part Montessori Cards (Amphibians)
- Frog Life Cycle Poster and Worksheet
- French + Spanish Flashcards

☐ "Pond Sensory Bin" (search Pinterest)
☐ Nature's Playground (pg 42-45)

3 Day Schedule

Day 1

- ☐ Morning Basket: Include term reading, poem recitation, handicraft, and memory statement introduction
- ☐ Read <u>Over and Under the Pond</u> (Messner).
- ☐ Discuss the various amphibians found in the text.
- ☐ Outdoor Exploration: Discuss the idea of remembering what we see and "painting a picture" inside our minds. (Reference page 29)
- ☐ Look for signs of amphibians, exploring near waterways and under rocks and logs.
- ☐ Use the French or Spanish terms for frog, pond, and green as the opportunity presents itself.
- ☐ Recite the memory statement twice during your discussions.
- ☐ Sort amphibians from reptiles or identify and describe amphibians utilizing the 3-Part Montessori Cards.

Day 2

- ☐ Morning Basket: Include term reading, poem recitation, handicraft, practice memory statement
- ☐ Read an optional book of your choosing from the "book menu" for Unit 1.
- ☐ Begin your chosen activity for the unit: Set up the tadpole habitat, find a natural frog habitat, visit a pet store, or bring out the life cycle representations you purchased. Enjoy this exploration.
- ☐ Consider documenting in your <u>Nature Collection Journal</u>.
- ☐ Use the French or Spanish flashcards to review the foreign language terms. Use them naturally as you discuss the material.
- ☐ Play the "picture-painting" game again on a very small scale today, following your child's lead. (Page 29)
- ☐ Recite the memory statements twice during your discussions.

Day 3

- ☐ Morning Basket: Include term reading, poem recitation, handicraft
- ☐ Today, you will visit your first Walk/View of the year. Explain that you're going on a walk and will be practicing your "picture-painting" game in your minds. Once you've arrived at the walk leading to your view, play the "picture-painting" game once again. Make sure to do your own as an example. If you have a mini-perfectionist, feel free to make mistakes as you share what you remember in your mind. Keep your own example very simple to demonstrate the basics. See page 29 for pointers.
- ☐ After some time exploring and ONE "picture-painting" session, review your French/Spanish terms naturally in your discussions.
- ☐ Recite your memory statements during your discussions.
- ☐ Complete the Frog Life Cycle worksheet from the Bundle.

5 Day Schedule

Day 1
- ☐ Morning Basket: Include term reading, poem recitation, handicraft, and memory statement introduction
- ☐ Outdoor Exploration: Discuss the concept of remembering what we see and "painting a picture" inside of our minds. (Reference page 29)
- ☐ Use the foreign language terms during discussion and exploration, as appropriate.

Day 2
- ☐ Morning Basket: Include term reading, poem recitation, handicraft, practice memory statement
- ☐ Read Over and Under the Pond (Messner)
- ☐ Begin your chosen activity for the unit: Set up the tadpole habitat, find a natural frog habitat, visit a pet store, or bring out the life cycle representations you purchased.
- ☐ Play a "picture-painting" warm-up game or memory games. (page 29)

Day 3
- ☐ Morning Basket: Include term reading, poem recitation, handicraft
- ☐ Visit your Walk/View, practicing observation and remembering skills, reflecting child's level (page 29)
- ☐ Practice the memory statement during your discussions on the walk
- ☐ Use French/Spanish flashcards to practice new terms

Day 4
- ☐ Morning Basket: Include term reading, poem recitation, handicraft, and memory statements
- ☐ Read aloud an additional book from the "book menu" and discuss
- ☐ Outside exploration
- ☐ Use foreign language terms during discussion and exploration, as appropriate.
- ☐ Sort amphibians from reptiles and other animals using the 3-Part Montessori Cards from the Bundle

Day 5
- ☐ Morning Basket: Include term reading, poem recitation, handicraft, practice memory statement
- ☐ Continuing working on, visiting, or observing your frog project
- ☐ Sequence the frog life cycle cards from the Bundle
- ☐ Review French/Spanish terms with flashcards again
- ☐ Mentally "walk through" your Walk/View from Day 3 (depending upon level, prompting and helping as needed)

2 Week Schedule

Daily
- Morning Basket: Include term reading, poem recitation, handicraft, and memory statement introduction/practice
- Outside Exploration: Spend as much time outside daily in free exploration and collecting/observing flowers, trees, birds

Day 1
- Morning Basket
- Read Over and Under the Pond (Messner)
- Introduce new foreign language terms with flashcards (reviewing previously learned ones as well)
- Outside Exploration

Day 2
- Morning Basket
- Begin your chosen activity for the unit. Set up the tadpole habitat, find a natural frog habitat, visit a pet store, or bring out the life cycle representations you purchased.
- Outside Exploration

Day 3
- Morning Basket
- Play the "picture-painting" or other memory games today as a warm-up (page 29)
- Read a book from the "book menu" for Unit 1.
- Practice French or Spanish terms using flashcards.
- Outside Exploration

Day 4
- Morning Basket
- Visit the Walk/View for the first time, practicing observation and remembering skills, reflecting child's level
- Look for opportunities to drop "nature nuggets," utilize the memory statements, or practice foreign language terms

Day 5
- Morning Basket
- Continue observing the tadpole habitat.
- Read a book from the "book menu" for Unit 1.
- Sort amphibians from reptiles and other animals using the 3-Part Montessori Cards from the Bundle
- Outside Exploration

Day 6
- Morning Basket
- Review French/Spanish terms with flashcards again
- Mentally "walk through" your Walk/View from Day 4 to practice your remembering skills
- Outside Exploration

Day 7
- Morning Basket
- Sequence the frog life cycle cards from the Bundle
- Finalize any additional unit projects, review the parts of your frog metamorphosis set, or pay special attention to your tadpoles today
- Outside Exploration

Day 8
- Morning Basket
- Finalize any projects from unit
- Consider having your child share all they've learned via an oral or written narration with another family member
- Outside Exploration

©Gentle + Classical Nature

UNIT 2: FRESHWATER FISH

OVERVIEW

In Unit 1, we launched our exploration into God's creation by exploring the amazing world of amphibians. For this unit, we continue to hang out in local ponds or rivers by exploring the lives of the fish that inhabit them. In Term 2, there will be a completely separate set of units that focus on saltwater sea life. The focus this unit is on the function of fish gills. Obviously, this isn't specific to freshwater fish. However, in your reading selections, you can be guided by the focus on fish living in rivers and ponds versus the vast ocean life that will receive several weeks of attention in Term 2.

NATURE NUGGETS

https://easyscienceforkids.com/all-about-fish/
http://www.sciencekids.co.nz/sciencefacts/animals/fish.html

TEACHER NOTES

If you didn't have an opportunity to get started on your tadpole metamorphosis project last week, this is a perfect time to start. Don't stress out about "aligning" this unit's fish information with starting an amphibian project. Beginning the tadpole project at ANY time will be beneficial and give your child the opportunity to observe what he was previously learning about. Remember, education is a life- mixed up, messy, and beautiful.

The content in this unit's memory statements focuses on fish anatomy and the function of their gills, mainly answering the question, "How do fish breath in the water?" Other ideas for exploration would be reading about and studying the fish life cycle as well. Both sturgeon and catfish have interesting life cycles to read about. This link goes to a pdf download specific to these two species: http://bit.ly/fishLC

Looking Ahead: Unit 3 will cover aquatic arthropods— specifically dragonflies for the lower level. While you're exploring nature around ponds or waterways during this unit and observing fish, keep an eye out for the dragonfly in each of its developmental stages as well.

In the Gentle + Classical Nature Term 1 Bundle from the shop (LifeAbundantlyBlog.com/shop), there are 3-Part Montessori Cards related to several species of freshwater fish, a fish life cycle worksheet, and the French/Spanish vocabulary flash cards you'll need for this unit.

UNIT 2 ATTAINMENTS

Last week, in Unit 1, you had the opportunity to visit and explore the Walk/View that you chose to study with your child. In this unit, we will visit your "Body of Water" to observe for the first time.

Everything from the previous unit still applies. If you have a Level 1 child who is still in the early stages of being trained in the art of observing and remembering, continue to play the "picture-painting" game and other related memory games on a smaller scale- gradually building up these skills to develop their "remembering muscles." If memory is something your child struggles with, Gentle + Classical Preschool Level 2 includes specific auditory and visual memory exercises that are beneficial to all children.

In addition to visiting your "Body of Water" for the first of many viewings, you'll want to specifically look for an opportunity to mentally review the portions of the Walk/View that you worked on during Unit 1. Remember, per Miss Mason's warnings, this type of "mental viewing" is rather tiresome, so use it judiciously. You'll want to mentally walk through that first visit, to whatever extent your child is capable, just once in review before you visit it again. Your child may remember a number of details or draw a complete blank- both are fine and well within "normal," especially after just one visit. Make sure to keep playing memory-building games, modeling observation skills on daily Nature Explorations. You absolutely may have to train your child to SEE small, important details for quite some time. Everyone is different. Remember, Mama, the entire goal is the PROCESS, not the end result.

Aside from the viewing and reviewing of these attainments, we will be gathering our first nature collectible, to be identified and mounted in the Nature Collection Journal. The goal for Term 1 is 4 wildflowers, 2 trees, and the identification of 2 birds. This unit, we will gather/collect our first wildflower. However, depending upon when you begin this program, you might not have those available. Don't hesitate to change the order of this portion of the program. If you're in the midst of winter, consider beginning with observing a bird. Unit 6 on page 70 goes into more detail related to bird observations. (Pages 30-33 in this guide gives more detailed instruction on wildflowers and trees.)

Unit 2 Attainment Goals
- [ ] Visit the "Body of Water" you chose for Term 1; "picture-paint" with your child on this visit
- [ ] Mentally review your Walk/View visit from last unit
- [ ] Collect the first wildflower specimen and add it to your Nature Collection Journal
- [ ] Begin/Continue Term Project #1 (weeks 1-6): Tadpole Metamorphosis
- [ ] Continue daily recitation of your first chosen nature poem
- [ ] Continue daily practice of chosen handicraft

UNIT 2 AT-A-GLANCE

Unit 2 Attainment Goals
- ☐ Visit the "Body of Water" you chose for Term 1; "picture-paint" with your child on this visit
- ☐ Mentally review your Walk/View visit from last unit
- ☐ Collect the first wildflower specimen and add it to your Nature Collection Journal
- ☐ Begin/Continue Term Project #1 (weeks 1-6): Tadpole Metamorphosis
- ☐ Continue daily recitation of your first chosen nature poem
- ☐ Continue daily practice of chosen handicraft

FOREIGN LANGUAGE

SPANISH	FRENCH
fish- el pez	fish- le poisson
egg- el huevo	egg- l'oeuf
water- el agua	water- l'eau

MEMORY STATEMENTS

LEVEL 1
Fish swim in the water and breathe through gills.

LEVEL 2
Fish have gills that extract oxygen from the water around them.

LEVEL 3
Combine Level 1 & 2 OR:
Fish are vertebrate animals that lay eggs for reproduction and have gills that extract oxygen from the water around them.

LITERATURE SELECTIONS

LEVEL 1
Term Reading 1: Frog and Toad Storybook Treasury (Lobel)- 22 pages per unit

Highly Recommended:
Over and Under the Pond (Messner)
Nature Anatomy (Rothman) (p206-207)

Optional Book Menu:
One Fish, Two Fish, Red Fish, Blue Fish (Dr. Seuss)
A Fish Out of Water (Palmer)
In the Small, Small Pond (Fleming) *super short
Pond Circle (Franco)
Fish Had a Wish (Garland) *beginning reader

LEVEL 2
Term 1 Reading: Among the Pond People (Pierson)- 16 Pages per unit/3-5 pages per day

Highly Recommended:
Same as Level 1 Reading

Optional Book Menu:
One Small Square: Pond (Silver)
Pond (LaMarche)
The Raft (LaMarche)

ACTIVITIES + FIELD TRIPS + EXPLORATIONS

KEYS TO REMEMBER

⚑ Nature exploration time is to be child-led with "key points" sown into their ready minds by Mom when the opportunity arises.

"All teaching of our children should be given reverently, with the humble sense that we are invited in this matter to co-operate with the Holy Spirit." -Charlotte Mason

FISH EXPLORATIONS

🌲 Research a little in advance and look for a local stream, creek, pond, river, or lake to visit.
🌲 Looking around the edge of the waterway closely will help you find small "fry" fish.
🌲 Plan a day of fishing with your family. If your family doesn't fish, maybe a friend or relative can help you get started.
🌲 Is there a local farmer's market or seafood market that you can tour?
🌲 Is there a fish farm in your area? Can you tour it or join in a local field trip?
🌲 Do you have an aquarium in your area to visit to view both fresh and saltwater fish? Many of them allow homeschoolers to coordinate field trips for reduced admission.
🌲 Here is a list of natural history museums in the US that may have exhibits specific to fish in your area: http://bit.ly/NatMusUS
🌲 Visit the local pet store for no-commitment observation.

EVEN MORE FUN!

Song: There are SEVERAL fish songs listed here: http://bit.ly/fishsongs
Activities: from Gentle + Classical Nature Term 1 Bundle
- Fish 3-Part Montessori Cards
- Frog Life Cycle Worksheet (if you're still working on your frog project)
- French + Spanish Flashcards

☐ "Pond Sensory Bin" (search Pinterest)
☐ This link has several super simple, crafty fish activities: http://bit.ly/fishcrafts
☐ Nature's Playground (pg 54-59)

UNIT 3: AQUATIC ARTHROPODS

OVERVIEW

In Unit 3, we continue to dwell in pond and lake habitats by exploring aquatic arthropods. Arthropoda is actually an extremely large and broad classification of invertebrates. We narrow in this unit on arthropods that live in waterways. In several later units in Term 1, we will learn about other kinds of arthropods (insects and arachnids). The memory statement for Level 1 zeros in on dragonflies. For youngest learners, these little magical flying creatures are a great example of an arthropod that dwells in our waterways. Dragonflies are fun to watch and have extremely interesting life cycles. For Levels 2-3, we focus more on arthropods in general, including the process of molting. As always, feel free to mix and match levels based upon your children's interests and your priorities.

NATURE NUGGETS

http://www.biology4kids.com/files/invert_arthropod.html
http://www.softschools.com/facts/animals/arthropods_facts/3225/
https://www.ducksters.com/animals/dragonfly.php

TEACHER NOTES

One thing to note is that, while this unit is focused on freshwater arthropods, only 3% of insects (25,000 to 30,000 species) are aquatic or have aquatic larval stages, and most of these are freshwater, not marine. In Term 2, where we explore oceans, we will specifically focus on marine arthropods in the subphylum Crustacea.

Foreign Language Note: One important thing to notice about practicing Spanish and/or French with your little one is that the article (el/la/le) is included in this curriculum alongside the noun. For your reference, "la" is feminine in both Spanish and French. "El" is the masculine form in Spanish, and "le" is the masculine form in French. As your child grows older and continues to study these languages more formally, they will be equipped with a GREAT advantage to already know the articles (and gender) for these nouns. Even if they don't understand it now, making sure to include that article as you practice them will help set a sturdy foundation for their future foreign language development.

If you are continuing to study the metamorphosis of frogs for Project 1, it's a great idea to have your child sketch (based upon level) what he is observing as the tadpoles make their gradual change into a frog. Verbally modeling these observations to your child is a great opportunity to demonstrate these skills and will help them in their attainments as well.

In the Gentle + Classical Nature Term 1 Bundle from the shop (LifeAbundantlyBlog.com/shop), there are 3-Part Montessori Cards related to several species of arthropods, a dragon fly life cycle worksheet, and the French/Spanish vocabulary flashcards you'll need for this unit.

UNIT 3 ATTAINMENTS

The fun really begins! This unit, we will REVISIT our Walk/View for the term. This is a fantastic opportunity to see what you remembered correctly, fill in gaps in both of your memories, and observe new things that you didn't notice the first time.

Has the temperature changed much?
Has the plant life changed in any way?
Is the animal life more active or less active?
Are you visiting at the same time of day? If not, how is the lighting different?
Is today a windy day or calm? How does it compare to your last visit?

One suggestion is to focus upon one small area of the overall view and work to paint that upon your mind, rather than the entire view at once. The younger your child or the more they might struggle to stay focused on this task, the smaller the area you should attend to. Maybe there are curves in the path you could note, a particularly interesting rock or tree, or the sounds of a stream nearby. Whatever it is that's notable, keep modeling for your child to the extent that they need you to.

You'll also want to review the "Body of Water" you visited for the first time during the last unit. Have a small review "picture-painting" session of what you observed at the "Body of Water" on a day separate from revisiting your Walk/View. It's best to maintain a consistent awareness of not overdoing things in one day.

Since you began your plant collection last unit, this week you will want to take time to visit that first wildflower again. You can do this in person or review via the specimen you collected. Opt for in-person as much as possible, so that you can further reflect upon and observe the habitat in which it grows as well.

Next unit, you will want to visit and collect the first tree you'd like to study. If you haven't chosen and located that already, this is a great time to do that.

Unit 3 Attainment Goals
- [ ] Revisit Term 1 Walk/View; continue to "picture-paint"
- [ ] Mentally review last unit's "Body of Water"
- [ ] Review the first wildflower specimen you collected in person or in your Nature Collection Journal
- [ ] Begin/Continue Term Project #1 (weeks 1-6): Tadpole Metamorphosis
- [ ] Continue daily recitation of chosen nature poem
- [ ] Continue daily practice of chosen handicraft

UNIT 3 AT-A-GLANCE

Unit 3 Attainment Goals
- ☐ Revisit Term 1 Walk/View; continue to "picture-paint"
- ☐ Mentally review last unit's "Body of Water"
- ☐ Review the first wildflower specimen you collected in person or in your Nature Collection Journal
- ☐ Begin/Continue Term Project #1 (weeks 1-6): Tadpole Metamorphosis
- ☐ Continue daily recitation of chosen nature poem
- ☐ Continue daily practice of chosen handicraft

FOREIGN LANGUAGE

SPANISH	FRENCH
insect- el insecto	insect- l'insecte
dragonfly- la libélula	dragonfly- la libellule
wing- el ala	wing- l'aile

MEMORY STATEMENTS

LEVEL 1	LEVEL 2	LEVEL 3
Dragonflies live underwater before they grow wings and fly.	All arthropods have an exoskeleton, which they shed and regrow.	Combine Level 2 with the following: This process is called molting.

LITERATURE SELECTIONS

LEVEL 1
Term Reading 1: Frog and Toad Storybook Treasury (Lobel)- 22 pages per unit

Highly Recommended:
Over and Under the Pond (Messner)
Nature Anatomy (Rothman) (p89-95)

Optional Book Menu:
Are You a Dragonfly? (Allen)
Pond Walk (Wallace)
Dragonflies (Rice)

LEVEL 2
Term 1 Reading: Among the Pond People (Pierson)- 16 Pages per unit/3-5 pages per day

Highly Recommended:
Same as Level 1 Reading

Optional Book Menu:
Dragonflies of North America (Biggs)
Soar High Dragonfly (Bestor)
The Web at Dragonfly Pond (Ellis)
Eliza and the Dragonfly (Rinehart)
The Dragonfly Door (Adams)

ACTIVITIES + FIELD TRIPS + EXPLORATIONS

KEYS TO REMEMBER

🍂 You may want to read <u>Over and Under the Pond</u> once per unit, once every other unit, or multiple times each unit. There's no wrong way to utilize this amazing book!

AQUATIC ARTHROPOD EXPLORATIONS

🌲 Research a little in advance and look for a local stream, creek, pond, river, or lake to visit.

🌲 Various species of dragonflies mate and lay their eggs in very different locations in water. You'll be hard-pressed to find dragonfly eggs. However, you might luck out and find nymphs.

🌲 This website (http://bit.ly/drangonflypic) has a variety of helpful images and resources to help you identify nymphs or find molted exoskeletons.

🌲 What other arthropods might you find local to your area that leave a visible molted shell? In the southeast US, locusts and cicadas are plentiful and leave very easy to find molts behind.

🌲 Are you interested in branching out from dragonflies? Other aquatic arthropods are: whirligig, caddisfly, crayfish, and mosquitoes.

🌲 Crayfish can be found in many ponds and lakes. They can even be collected and observed as pets. This link (http://bit.ly/crayfishpet) has some great information about the care and keeping of crayfish.

🌲 There are quite a few insectariums and collections all over the US. This link lists 10: http://bit.ly/insectzoo Search for similar resources and collections in your local area.

EVEN MORE FUN!

<u>Video</u>: This is a really vivid, short video on Youtube: http://bit.ly/DFVideo1
<u>Activities</u>: from <u>Gentle + Classical Nature</u> Term 1 Bundle
- Arthropod 3-Part Montessori Cards
- Dragonfly Life Cycle Worksheet
- French + Spanish Flashcards

☐ Try using rocks, sticks, nuts, moss, and more found objects to build your own dragonflies or other arthropods.

☐ This q-tip dragonfly craft would be really fun and great for fine motor skills (http://bit.ly/qtipDF). Angela at ProjectsWithKids.com also has a free template to use for this craft. Otherwise, a quick search of "Dragonfly Activities" on Pinterest yields some really simple results!

☐ <u>Nature's Playground</u> (pg 170-171)

UNIT 4: WATERBIRDS (FRESHWATER FOCUS)

OVERVIEW

In Unit 4, we move out from under the water to observe and learn about birds that live in and beside the water. For Level 1 learners, we focus just on naming a few waterfowl that live near freshwater sources while for Levels 2 and 3, we turn our attention to the insulating properties of their plumage. Later in this term, we will focus more upon typical forest or "backyard birds." In Term 2, we will turn our attention to coastal birds. However, if you live in an area that's predominantly coastal, focusing on coastal birds twice might be worthwhile. It's important to remember to 1) use your local resources and 2) focus your exploration upon concepts that are close-to-home for these young ages. Something they have the opportunity to explore in person is significantly more beneficial than images in a book or video, especially for this age group.

NATURE NUGGETS

http://www.birdsinbackyards.net/birds/featured/Water-birds
https://easyscienceforkids.com/all-about-freshwater-birds/
http://www.waterencyclopedia.com/A-Bi/Birds-Aquatic.html

TEACHER NOTES

Waterbirds alone are so diverse and interesting, you won't quickly run out of observations to discuss. For this unit in particular, I would encourage you to work very hard to find a way to observe a variety of waterbirds for as long and often as possible. There is a very helpful item called Bird Observation Pack found at LifeAbundantlyBlog.com/shop

Ideas for discussion:
- Plumage colors
- Purposes of different kinds of feathers (Nature Anatomy page 168)
- Diet variations (fish vs algae)
- Methods of hunting (diving vs wading)
- Shape and color of beaks
- Bird calls
- Variations between male and female of a species
- Length of legs
- Migratory or not
- And on and on and on....

I'll share more bird study ideas in the section titled "Waterbird Explorations" in a few pages.

If you are continuing to observe frog metamorphosis, I would love to see your images on Instagram! You can tag me (@lifeabundantly_blog) and use tag #gentleclassicalnature.

Looking Ahead: In Unit 7, we will begin Project 2 of the term- butterfly metamorphosis. The caterpillars can be very sensitive to extreme heat and cold, so you might want to begin considering now when you will begin this project. We've always purchased the Insect Lore Deluxe Butterfly Garden with Caterpillars from Amazon. You actually receive the kit with the net and related materials directly from Amazon but receive a certificate with a code for ordering the larvae directly from Insect Lore. They will only be able to ship the larvae when they won't be exposed to extreme temperatures, so keep that in mind. You can get further details about them at www.InsectLore.com.

In the Gentle + Classical Nature Term 1 Bundle from the shop (LifeAbundantlyBlog.com/shop), there are 3-Part Montessori Cards related to several species of water birds and the French/Spanish vocabulary flashcards you'll need for this unit.

UNIT 4 ATTAINMENTS

In this unit, we will circle back and visit our "Body of Water" for the second time this term. It may be helpful to take a camera with you if your child is struggling to remember details accurately or is bothered by not knowing whether he is "right" about something he saw. You may also want to consider having a special collection of found objects just for this location. Each time you return, you can add new mementos of this special place. Have you child decorate a special box just for this purpose or designate a special nature table.

While we are definitely aiming to help our child develop her observation skills and sharpen her memory, we also want these visits and locations to be special and memorable from an emotional perspective as well. Miss Mason often wrote about how these mental images can later bring us peace and joy when we may need it most, indicating that this experience is as much about creating pleasant memories as it is about developing skills.

Not only are you training your child in mental skills, but you're also helping her build a storehouse of treasured memories... so be sure to enjoy these visits. Bring snacks, blankets, comfortable clothes, magnifying glasses, jars for collections, pencils and paper, camera- whatever your family needs in order to settle in and help this environment become an extension of home. Choosing a time that you won't be rushed to get finished or get to an appointment is incredibly important.

We and our children need opportunities to just be present in God's creation with not much agenda other than absorbing the sights, sounds, smells and wonder. While you'll use these visits as an opportunity for training your children in "picture-painting," when they become fully acquainted with this piece of land and spend many hours dwelling in it, "picture-painting" it will be no more of a concerted effort than remembering their room at home.

In this unit, your little one will visit and collect pieces of the first tree for this term. Just like with the wildflower from Unit 2, you'll want to find a tree that's convenient to your home and that you can visit as often as possible. It doesn't have to be a big tree! If resources are limited, you can even use a shrub. The point is that your child would get intimately acquainted with this species and be able to identify it anywhere. See page 33 for a refresher on collecting and visiting this specimen.

Unit 4 Attainment Goals
- [ ] Revisit Term 1 "Body of Water"; continue to "picture-paint"
- [ ] Mentally review last unit's Walk/View
- [ ] Collect your first tree parts and mount in your Nature Collection Journal
- [ ] Review your wildflower in person or via the Nature Collection Journal
- [ ] Begin/Continue Term Project #1 (weeks 1-6): Tadpole Metamorphosis
- [ ] Continue daily recitation of your first chosen nature poem
- [ ] Continue daily practice of chosen handicraft

UNIT 4 AT-A-GLANCE

Unit 4 Attainment Goals
- Revisit Term 1 "Body of Water"; continue to "picture-paint"
- Mentally review last unit's Walk/View
- Collect your first tree parts and mount in your Nature Collection Journal
- Review your wildflower in person or via the Nature Collection Journal
- Begin/Continue Term Project #1 (weeks 1-6): Tadpole Metamorphosis
- Continue daily recitation of your first chosen nature poem
- Continue daily practice of chosen handicraft

FOREIGN LANGUAGE

SPANISH	FRENCH
duck- el pato	duck- le canard
goose- el ganso	goose- l'oie
bird- el pajaro	bird- l'oiseau

MEMORY STATEMENTS

LEVEL 1
Ducks, geese, and swans (are waterbirds that) live near rivers and lakes. *portion in parentheses is an optional addition

LEVEL 2
Waterbirds have thick down feathers which insulate their bodies.

LEVEL 3
Waterbirds have thick down feathers which insulate their bodies, and most have bills and legs adapted to feed in water and dive from the surface to catch prey.

LITERATURE SELECTIONS

LEVEL 1
Term Reading 1: Frog and Toad Storybook Treasury (Lobel)- 22 pages per unit

Highly Recommended:
Over and Under the Pond (Messner)
Nature Anatomy (Rothman) (Chapter 6 in full)

Optional Book Menu:
The Ugly Duckling (Anderson)
All Night Near the Water (Arnosky)
Have You Seen My Duckling? (Tafuri)
Petunia (Duvoisin)
Little Swan (London)

LEVEL 2
Term 1 Reading: Among the Pond People (Pierson)- 16 Pages per unit/3-5 pages per day

Highly Recommended:
Same as Level 1 Reading

Optional Book Menu:
Make Way for Duckling (McCloskey)
The Story of Ping (Flack)
The Tale of Jemima Puddle Duck (Potter)
Feathers: Not Just for Flying (Stewart)
Rechenka's Eggs (Polacco)
Henry the Impatient Heron (Love)

ACTIVITIES + FIELD TRIPS + EXPLORATIONS

KEYS TO REMEMBER

Have fun, Mama! Sometimes we can get wound a little tight, trying to get everything "in" during busy days. Remember, as Sarah MacKenzie famously said, your curriculum is a "best guess." This curriculum is meant to be a guide, a menu to choose from, not a rulebook to dictate days. Keep at it, but enjoy the process!

WATERBIRD EXPLORATIONS

🌲 Research a little in advance and look for a local stream, creek, pond, river, or lake to visit.

🌲 As you (hopefully) have a chance to explore a local waterway and get to see a variety of waterfowl in their natural habitat, here are some suggested questions to prompt thought and observation in your child. However, make sure to leave plenty of room for his own explorations and observations without leading as well:

- ❓ Can you notice a difference between the male and female's feathers? Why are they different?
- ❓ How long do you think the duck (or goose) can hold its breath underwater?
- ❓ Do you think their feathers get heavy and soaked with water like a towel?
- ❓ Why do you think the duck has short legs but herons (flamingos, etc) have long legs?
- ❓ What is the most interesting thing you notice about the _____?

🌲 One place to often see baby ducks or geese is a local farmer's co-op or feed store.

🌲 Of course, local zoos, nature preserves, and water preserves will host an interesting assortment of feathered friends as well.

🌲 One particular topic to ponder and discuss is wildlife conservation; discuss and explore the ecological impact pollution has on waterways. How does pollution from a factory make its way to ponds and lakes? How does that affect the food chain? Here's a great website that walks you through what water pollution is and how it affects all wildlife in the food chain: http://bit.ly/waterpollution1

EVEN MORE FUN!

> **Note**: According to specialists it is best NOT to feed wild animals (including water fowl) bread or other human foods.

Game: Duck, Duck Goose
Activities: from Gentle + Classical Nature Term 1 Bundle
- Montessori 3-Part Cards
- French + Spanish Flashcards

☐ If you have the ability to do so, borrow an incubator and fertilized eggs and wait for the day that the babies hatch! Some 4H programs or farm programs in your area may loan these out. You don't have to commit to owning the birds but get the opportunity to watch them hatch and care for them in those first few days. Plus, you can "candle" the eggs to watch the embryos grow.

☐ Search "assortment of feathers" on Amazon to get a small variety for crafts or to play on your light table.

UNIT 5: FRESHWATER MAMMALS

OVERVIEW

Who does not obsessively fall in love with manatees when they first see these magnificent and gentle creatures? There are several, diverse species of mammals that call rivers and lakes home that are incredibly interesting. In this unit we will focus on listing a few freshwater mammals for Level 1, then focus in more specifically on the definition of "mammal" for Levels 2 and 3.

NATURE NUGGETS

https://en.wikipedia.org/wiki/Aquatic_mammal

TEACHER NOTES

There are a variety of aquatic mammals that call freshwater locations home- but they are a little harder to find than a goose or duck from last unit. Some species include: river dolphin, manatee, otter, hippo, muskrat, capybara, beaver, platypus, shrew, moose, and polar bear.

If you didn't dive much into conservation in the last unit, I encourage you to set aside some time this unit. I'll list some resources in Explorations.

If you are continuing to observe frog metamorphosis, I would love to see your images on Instagram. You can tag me (@lifeabundantly_blog) and use tag #gentleclassicalnature.

Looking Ahead: In Unit 7, we will begin Project 2 of the term- butterfly metamorphosis. The caterpillars can be very sensitive to extreme heat and cold, so you might want to begin considering now when you will begin this project. We've always purchased the Insect Lore Deluxe Butterfly Garden with Caterpillars. You actually receive the kit with the net and related materials, but receive a certificate with a code for ordering the larvae. They will only be able to ship the larvae when they won't be exposed to extreme temperatures, so keep that in mind. You can get further details from them at www.InsectLore.com.

In the Gentle + Classical Nature Term 1 Bundle from the shop (LifeAbundantlyBlog.com/shop), there are Montessori 3-part cards related to several species of aquatic mammals and the French/Spanish vocabulary flash cards you'll need for this unit.

UNIT 5 ATTAINMENTS

In this unit, we will circle back and visit our Walk/View for another look. Many of the same notes from last unit apply. Make sure to keep your focus on the relationship with your child and with the environment rather than on training.

Also, set time aside to remember the "Body of Water" that you visited for the second time last unit. Can your child recall any more details than the first time? Are particular things coming freshly to mind? Continue modeling and playing memory games as needed. While "picture-painting" is a bit laborious and should be used judiciously, basic matching games are brain-training fun for your kids. Feel free to make memory-building games a daily part of your homeschool. The more you train their minds to attend and retain in these early years when their brains are still developing so rapidly, the more time you will save yourself (and your child) in the future!

In this unit, we switch gears from collecting wildflowers and trees, to finding and observing the first bird of Term 1. You likely had an opportunity to see a few birds last unit. If so, it's a great idea for one of those species to be your bird for observation, especially if you have easy access to their location. However, any of us can lure birds our way with feeders and flowers. Ideally, you want to choose a species that's local to you. The ability to be frequently acquainted gives your child ample opportunity to study how the bird flies, hunts, sings, and builds nests. See pages 34 and 70 for more details and game ideas for observing bird habits.

Make sure to frequently visit your first tree and wildflower to observe how they're changing as the weather changes. If that's not doable, then pull out your Nature Collection Journal a few days each week to review the parts you collected.

Unit 5 Attainment Goals
- [ ] Revisit Term 1 Walk/View, Continue to "picture-paint"
- [ ] Mentally review last unit's "Body of Water" that you revisited
- [ ] Review (in person or in the Nature Collection Journal) the tree and flower you've collected
- [ ] Search for, observe, and identify your first bird
- [ ] Begin/Continue Term Project #1 (weeks 1-6): Tadpole Metamorphosis
- [ ] Choose a NEW poem to begin reciting for the next 4 units.
- [ ] Continue daily practice of chosen handicraft

UNIT 5 AT-A-GLANCE

Unit 5 Attainment Goals
- [ ] Revisit Term 1 Walk/View, Continue to "picture-paint"
- [ ] Mentally review last unit's "Body of Water" that you revisited
- [ ] Review (in person or in the Nature Collection Journal) the tree and flower you've collected
- [ ] Search for, observe, and identify your first bird
- [ ] Begin/Continue Term Project #1 (weeks 1-6): Tadpole Metamorphosis
- [ ] Choose a NEW poem to begin reciting for the next 4 units.
- [ ] Continue daily practice of chosen handicraft

FOREIGN LANGUAGE

SPANISH	FRENCH
river- el rio	river- la riviere
air- el air	air- l'air
beaver- el castor	beaver- le castor

MEMORY STATEMENTS

LEVEL 1	LEVEL 2	LEVEL 3
Beavers, river otters, and manatees are aquatic mammals.	Aquatic mammals live in the water but breathe air and birth live young.	Beavers, river otters, and manatees are aquatic mammals which live in the water but breathe air and birth live young. Semi-aquatic mammals, like moose and polar bears, dwell in and feed partly from waterways.

LITERATURE SELECTIONS

LEVEL 1
Term Reading 1: Frog and Toad Storybook Treasury (Lobel)- 22 pages per unit

Highly Recommended:
Over and Under the Pond (Messner)
Nature Anatomy (Rothman) (pg 148-151)

Optional Book Menu:
Give a Moose a Muffin (Numeroff)
Looking for a Moose (Root)
Beavers (Gibbons)
A Drop Around the World (McKinney) *conservation
Sam the Sea Cow (Jacobs)

LEVEL 2
Term 1 Reading: Among the Pond People (Pierson)- 16 Pages per unit/3-5 pages per day

Highly Recommended:
Same as Level 1 Reading

Optional Book Menu:
Otters Underwater (Arnosky)
Riparia's River (Caduto)
National Geographic: Manatees (Marsh)
Henry the Manatee (Lawrence)
One Well (Strauss) *conservation

ACTIVITIES + FIELD TRIPS + EXPLORATIONS

KEYS TO REMEMBER

A little reminder from Miss Mason: "Every walk should offer some knotty problem for the children to think out, 'Why does that leaf float on the water, and this pebble sink?' and so on."

AQUATIC MAMMAL EXPLORATIONS

🌲 If you haven't had an opportunity yet, I encourage you (strongly!) to look for an opportunity to visit an aquarium, zoo, or natural history museum in your area that would include as many of these animals to view as possible.

🌲 This unit is an incredible time to dig further into conservation:

- Educate yourself then pass those "nuggets" along to your child while you are on your nature explorations.
- Look for opportunities to clean and protect any areas that you visit as you explore.
- See if you can identify signs of ecological damage or disruption to habitats when you observe your "Body of Water."
- Can you join groups in your area to visit and clean waterways?
- Is there a local conservation group or department that you can arrange a field trip to visit?
- Many museums and zoos that have local aquatic mammals have visual representations of garbage found in the animals' native habitats.
- This super simple experiment will help your students see how rainfall moves pollutants from one area to another, eventually ending up in rivers: http://bit.ly/watershedexp

🌲 Since we studied birds last unit, this is a great opportunity to discuss how mammals differ from the birds and amphibians that we have already studied- namely that mammals birth live young rather than eggs!

EVEN MORE FUN!

Activities: from Gentle + Classical Nature Term 1 Bundle
- Aquatic Mammal 3-Part Cards
- Ecology Poster
- French + Spanish Flashcards

☐ Consider building your own terrarium or diorama to represent all you've learned so far about freshwater wildlife. It could represent a pond, lake, river, or stream that you've had the opportunity to visit. Toob animals fit these well!

☐ Build your own beaver dam! A quick look on Pinterest will give you several ideas to help you get started. It could be on a very small scale in a casserole dish or you could make an edible one- out of peanut butter and pretzel sticks!

☐ Nature's Playground (p180)

UNIT 6: REPTILES

OVERVIEW

The reptilia class is a vast topic... and a fascinating one at that! In Level 1, we will memorize a few common reptiles to help our little ones understand that reptiles can still be very different. In level 2 and 3, we will focus on the ectothermic nature of reptiles along with a few other specific facts about reptiles. As usual, our foreign language terms will reflect that which we are studying in our Nature Focus.

NATURE NUGGETS

https://www.ducksters.com/animals/reptiles.php

TEACHER NOTES

This topic is another which is so diverse, it's truly owed weeks and weeks of study. Keep in mind, just because you may have spent a week on a prior topic doesn't mean you can't dive in and dwell in each particular subject as long as you or your students would like. The beauty in home education is that ability to dwell in each particular topic until you get your fill before moving along. You never know what might spark a true passion in your child.

As with any unit, feel free to trade out terms in the level 1 memory statement- if you prefer to list chameleons instead of (or in addition to) alligators, be my guest!

Next unit, we will begin our second term project- butterfly metamorphosis. Don't forget (weather permitting) to order your caterpillars as soon as possible.

In our science spine (highly recommended) reading, you will see us transitioning from Over and Under the Pond to Up in the Garden, Down in the Dirt. Both are a great fit for this unit. Read both or choose to move ahead to the next. We will use Up in the Garden, Down in the Dirt for several units, just as we have used Over and Under the Pond.

In the Gentle + Classical Nature Bundle, you will find Reptile 3-Part Cards that are very helpful this unit. You might utilize those as a sorting game, comparing the reptiles to amphibians, and observing the differences between the two. Remember that the instructions included with the 3-Part Montessori cards detail a variety of different ways to utilize these cards in your homeschool. You'll also find your French/Spanish Flashcards and a Butterfly Life Cycle sheet for your metamorphosis project coming up.

UNIT 6 ATTAINMENTS

In this unit, we will circle back and visit our "Body of Water" for another look. Many of the same notes from last unit apply.

Look for opportunities to engage with your "Body of Water" as much as possible- swimming, wading, skipping stones, fishing, and of course observing as much wildlife as possible. Continue to focus on one small portion at a time and meditate upon it, engaging your children with remembering games:

"Look at this portion of the pond. Do you see how there is a bunch of tall grass growing up in this corner, but not in the other? Let's look at it for a moment, then close our eyes and see if we can still see it. I can— can you?"

Watch for your child's response and be ready for mountains of specific encouragement, based on what they are able to recall. If they can't quite describe anything, continue to model, encouragingly:

"With my eyes closed, I can see the tall grass. The grass is taller than I am! It's green mostly but kind of brown at the top. When the wind blows, I can hear it making a sound... like walking on leaves in our yard. Can you hear that? I wonder if it's pokey or smooth. Maybe we should go see?"

Continue to not just work on these observing and remembering games but also interacting with the environment. Touch, smell, and bring home samples of as much as you can. You can curate a nature table dedicated to your "Body of Water" or Walk/View.

Recall things that YOU remember as much as possible— helping them to see how important and fun it is for us all to notice the world around us and to notice God's artistic and magnificent hand in it all. In this way, they get to experience the intrigue of being invited into another person's memories. When we model this type of sharing, it is a great encouragement and challenge to them.

You'll also want to make time to "picture-paint" your Walk/View that you revisited last week. What all can you remember? What can they remember? Was there a particular sight or smell that stays with them the strongest? The breeze, sunshine, or smells of the forest? Do they remember more of what they see, hear, smell, or touch? Talking through this together will help you learn more about how your child interacts with their environment.

Also, if this remembering is a point of continued struggle or even frustration, I encourage you to pause. You can stop all-together, back up and go back to more of the basic "picture-painting" games outlined on page 29, or take a camera along. Who says it's cheating to snap a few photos and see how much you can remember before glancing at the photos as a refresher? Some kids are scared to get things wrong, and would feel more confident sharing what they remember if they know they're "right" first. If this is your child, I encourage you to misremember a thing or two at times and allow them to help you remember it correctly— if you feel like they will catch your slip-up. Not only does it help them feel less intimidated if they aren't confident in their memories, but it also models humility— that we can work hard, make progress, and do our best all the while knowing we will never do it perfectly!

One last idea is that if you have a child who legitimately struggles with memory issues and has a related disability, don't hesitate to modify this entire process. One example would be that they photo-journal their Walk/View and "Body of Water." All children can benefit from building a scrapbook of images they take at these special locations. Alternatively, if you have blooming artists, allow them to sketch or paint as well. My daughter loves to "vlog" everything! There are a million different ways to help your child become deeply acquainted with these locations. The more you vary their "mode" of contact, the more likely they will carry this experience deep in their hearts forever. **I'm a huge fan of doing things the Charlotte Mason way- but we have a ton of options that Miss Mason did not have. There's massive merit in training our children in attention and observation through this process- but don't allow the ideal way to become a stumbling block to your child's experiences (and yours!).**

This unit, we will not be adding to our Nature Collection Journal. This is a nice opportunity to pause and just keep visiting, discussing, drawing, and interacting with the tree and wildflower you've collected so far.

Also, don't forget our bird we added last week! Can you take a special expedition to scout out this new friend? What else can you learn about this species by observing it? Especially for children who are 7+, it's a wonderful idea to learn as much about this species from their OWN observations before doing a massive amount of research. Then, once you begin to look up this species and really learn about it, they can see how right they were!

Points to ponder when observing their bird:
- Can we see the difference in the coloring of the male and female?
- Do they live in pairs, seem to be loners, or stay in a large flock?
- What different types of sounds do they make?
- Can we find a pattern as to why they make one sound and, at other times, make a different sound?
- Is their coloring, behavior, or call altered by the time of day or temperature outside?
- Can we find their nest?
- Is it high in a tree or low on the ground?
- Who would their natural predators be?
- Can we determine what they prefer to eat: worms and bugs or berries and seeds?
- If you have close access to your species, try offering a few different seed varieties in a feeder outside your window. Which option is this specie's favorite?

Unit 6 Attainment Goals

- [ ] Revisit Term 1 "Body of Water", Continue to "picture-paint"
- [ ] Mentally review last unit's Walk/View that you revisited
- [ ] Review (in person or in the <u>Nature Collection Journal</u>) the tree and flower you've collected
- [ ] Make a special expedition to visit and observe your first bird specimen from last unit
- [ ] Finish up Term Project #1 (weeks 1-6): Tadpole Metamorphosis
- [ ] Continue reciting your second poem of the term
- [ ] Continue daily practice of chosen handicraft

UNIT 6 AT-A-GLANCE

Unit 6 Attainment Goals
- Revisit Term 1 "Body of Water", Continue to "picture-paint"
- Mentally review last unit's Walk/View that you revisited
- Review (in person or in the Nature Collection Journal) the tree and flower you've collected
- Make a special expedition to visit and observe your first bird specimen
- Finish up Term Project #1 (weeks 1-6): Tadpole Metamorphosis
- Continue reciting your second poem of the term
- Continue daily practice of chosen handicraft

FOREIGN LANGUAGE

SPANISH	FRENCH
snake- la serpiente	snake- le serpent
turtle- la tortuga	turtle- la tortue
alligator- el caiman	alligator- l'alligator

MEMORY STATEMENTS

LEVEL 1
Alligators, snakes, and turtles are reptiles.

LEVEL 2
Reptiles are cold-blooded (ectothermic) and lay eggs.

LEVEL 3
Alligators, snakes, and turtles are reptiles. Reptiles are cold-blooded (ectothermic), lay eggs, and are covered in scales or have a bony external plate or shell.

LITERATURE SELECTIONS

LEVEL 1
Term Reading 1: Frog and Toad Storybook Treasury (Lobel)- 22 pages per unit

Highly Recommended:
Up in the Garden, Down in the Dirt (Messner)
Over and Under the Pond (Messner)
Nature Anatomy (Rothman) (pg 142-143; 153)

Optional Book Menu:
The Mixed Up Chameleon (Carle)
The Greedy Python (Carle)
Turtle Splash (Falwell)
The Snake Who Said Shhhh (Parachini)

LEVEL 2
Term 1 Reading: Among the Pond People (Pierson)- 16 Pages per unit/3-5 pages per day

Highly Recommended:
Same as Level 1 Reading

Optional Book Menu:
Snakes, Salamanders, and Lizards: Take-Along Guide (Burns)
Snakes (Gibbons)
An Extraordinary Egg (Lioni)
Cornelius (Lioni)
Alligators and Crocodiles (Gibbons)
Verdi (Cannon)

ACTIVITIES + FIELD TRIPS + EXPLORATIONS

KEYS TO REMEMBER

Have fun! That's probably the best reminder I can give you after a few weeks of digging into this program and into nature. Do what works for you. Don't be afraid to experiment!

REPTILE EXPLORATIONS

🌲 If you haven't had an opportunity yet, I encourage you (strongly!) to look for an opportunity to visit an aquarium, zoo, or natural history museum in your area that would include as many of these animals to view as possible. Go as often as you can!

🌲 A visit to the pet store is a great (no obligation) way to see a variety of species of reptiles.

🌲 What's the difference between a crocodile and an alligator? This would be a great "research" topic for your level 2 students. Maybe they could do an oral presentation about what they learn or build a visual display outlining the differences and similarities.

🌲 Why do snakes shed their skin? How and how often does this process take place? Do other reptiles also shed? YouTube has some great videos that explain this.

🌲 On a nature exploration, have your kids keep an eye out for any type of reptile they can identify. Can they find tracks from any type of small reptile or where a snake may have been? What about turtles on a log in a pond or lake? (Be aware, in N America, cottonmouths- aka water moccasins- are EXTREMELY venomous. Take proper precautions around bodies of water.)

🌲 How do reptiles survive during winter? This is a great opportunity to read, discuss, and watch documentaries about the adaptations that animals make in order to survive freezing temperatures. How have reptiles adapted to cold environments? What is hibernation?

🌲 Based upon your family's beliefs about evolution, you can also explore how birds (and dinosaurs) are classified as reptiles. While one classification system (the oldest, by Carrolus Linnaeus) is based on characteristics of each species (and grouping them thusly, which means that birds are not classified as reptiles as they have no scales and aren't ectothermic), the newer classification system (by Willi Hennig) uses ancestors (i.e. evolution) to determine how animals are related. The thesis being that birds and modern reptiles evolved from dinosaur and dinosaur predecessors in some manner. According to this classification system, birds are more closely related to reptiles (in particular, crocodiles) than any other group.

EVEN MORE FUN!

<u>Activities</u>: from <u>Gentle + Classical Nature</u> Term 1 Bundle
- Reptile Montessori 3-Part Cards
- French + Spanish Flashcards

📖 Play a sorting game with the 3-Part cards. Two great ideas would be to sort amphibians from reptiles or to sort cold-blooded (ectotherm) from warm-blooded animals (endotherms).

UNIT 7: BIRDS (INLAND)

OVERVIEW

We took a few moments in the last unit to really dive into all there is to observe and learn about birds under our attainments. They are truly fascinating in so many ways. In this unit, we will choose our second bird to observe and learn about for the term. We will also focus in on birds that choose the forest, mountains, prairie, or desert as their habitat.

NATURE NUGGETS

http://www.sciencekids.co.nz/sciencefacts/animals/bird.html
https://www.coolkidfacts.com/bird-facts/

TEACHER NOTES

In this unit (weather permitting!), it's time to get started with our second term project: caterpillar metamorphosis. If you haven't already ordered your caterpillars and enclosure, now is the time to get to it. As a reminder, if you order via Amazon (Nature Lore), they will mail you the enclosure and a code. You then have to use the code on their website to have the caterpillars shipped to you.

If this isn't a great time of year, just feel free to put a pin in this. While the project is incredibly rewarding, fun, and educational, WHEN you do it is absolutely immaterial. As a matter of fact, we do this each year in our home, unrelated to anything we are studying. It's THAT marvelous and mind-blowing to watch those tiny caterpillars (that barely move for a few days!) begin to eat, get HUGE, build their chrysalis, and then, BAM! The best surprise in the world is to check on them one morning to find that there is an ACTUAL butterfly in the enclosure. The process of metamorphosis is still beyond my comprehension!

An alternative, just as was mentioned with the frogs, is to get a life cycle set from Safari LTD. This is definitely a less expensive option. You could supplement with some time lapse YouTube videos to get a fuller effect as well. Plus there are so many excellent books— of course!

Unit 9 is when we will really dive into learning about butterflies. Consider timing their release and your in-depth butterfly explorations around that unit. In summer, you can expect the larva/caterpillar and pupa/chrysalis stages to each take about 10 to 14 days. In winter, autumn, and spring, the process takes a lot longer, as it slows down in cool weather.

Heads Up: When the pupa is ready to hatch, the shell will be transparent, and you can see the dark colours of the butterfly's wings folded up inside. The transformation happens suddenly, and if you turn away for a few minutes, you will usually come back to find a butterfly.

UNIT 7 ATTAINMENTS

In this unit, we revisit our Walk/View for the term. If you need refreshers on your goals, reread the previous unit's notes that discuss the focus of developing a relationship with the space and building memories over the goal of "picture-painting" your vista. We want to always balance the educational benefits of our attainments with the relationships and memories we develop with our children. The love of wisdom is what we hope to cultivate in their hearts above all!

> If any of you lacks wisdom, you should ask God, who gives generously to all without finding fault, and it will be given to you. -James 1:5

As mentioned in the Teacher Notes, we will be choosing our second bird for the term. Then, from this point forward, we will seek out as many opportunities as possible, during our normal weekly routines, to seek out and observe our birds' behaviors, habitats, food choices, etc based on the many suggestions offered on page 71.

Also, as mentioned in the Teacher Notes, we are starting Term Project 2: Butterfly Metamorphosis. If you skipped the notes, it's a good idea to head back there to catch up.

This unit, we will not be adding to our Nature Collection Journal aside from adding any feathers, pictures, or drawings of your two birds that you're observing for the term. This is a nice unit to take a pause and just keep visiting, discussing, drawing, and interacting with the tree and wildflower you've collected so far.

Unit 7 Attainment Goals
- [ ] Revisit Term 1 Walk/View; Continue to "picture-paint"
- [ ] Mentally review Term 1 "Body of Water" that you revisited last unit
- [ ] Review (in person or in the Nature Collection Journal) the tree and flower you've collected
- [ ] Make a special expedition to visit and observe your second bird specimen, keeping an eye out for your first specimen as well
- [ ] Begin Term Project #2: Butterfly Metamorphosis
- [ ] Continue reciting your second poem of the term
- [ ] Continue daily practice of chosen handicraft

UNIT 7 AT-A-GLANCE

Unit 7 Attainment Goals
- Revisit Term 1 Walk/View; Continue to "picture-paint"
- Mentally review Term 1 "Body of Water" that you revisited last unit
- Review (in person or in the Nature Collection Journal) the tree and flower you've collected
- Make a special expedition to visit and observe your second bird specimen, keeping an eye out for your first specimen as well
- Begin Term Project #2: Butterfly Metamorphosis
- Continue reciting your second poem of the term
- Continue daily practice of chosen handicraft

FOREIGN LANGUAGE

SPANISH	FRENCH
feather- la pluma	feather- la plume
Review wing, bird, and egg from earlier units.	Review wing, bird, and egg from earlier units.

MEMORY STATEMENTS

LEVEL 1	LEVEL 2	LEVEL 3
Birds have feathers, wings, and hollow bones and lay eggs.	Birds are warm-blooded vertebrates (endothermic) with feathers, wings, and hollow bones.	Birds, which lay eggs for reproduction, are endothermic vertebrates with feathers, wings, and hollow bones.

LITERATURE SELECTIONS

LEVEL 1
Term Reading 1: Frog & Toad Storybook Treasury (Lobel)- 22 pages per unit

Highly Recommended:
Up in the Garden, Down in the Dirt (Messner)
Nature Anatomy (Rothman) (Chapter 6)

Optional Book Menu:
A Nest is Noisy (Aston)
An Egg is Quiet (Aston)
Beautiful Birds (Roussen)
Mama Built a Little Nest (Ward)
Feathers for Lunch (Ehlert)

LEVEL 2
Term 1 Reading: Among the Pond People (Pierson)- 16 Pages per unit/3-5 pages per day

Highly Recommended:
Same as Level 1 Reading

Optional Book Menu:
The Burgess Bird Book for Children (Burgess)
The Boy Who Drew Birds (Davies)
Feathers- Not Just for Flying (Stewart)
Take Along Guide: Birds, Nests, & Eggs (Boring)
How Do Birds Find Their Way? (Gans)
Albert (Napoli)

ACTIVITIES + FIELD TRIPS + EXPLORATIONS

KEYS TO REMEMBER

Nothing special this unit, friend. Keep on, keeping on!

BIRD EXPLORATIONS

🌲 Page 71 has great questions to ask to encourage your student to really look at birds and all that they do with fresh eyes.

🌲 Many zoos and natural history museums have aviaries as well.

🌲 Take a walk! Nature exploration (daily if possible) is always a part of this program. Fortunately, most of us live where we can observe some species of bird just by stepping outside our doors. Most often, no big field trip is required. Careful observation and conversation about birds will lead to more understanding than anything else.

🌲 In Alabama, we have a raptor rescue (Southeastern Raptor Center). It's possible that you have something similar in your area. This is a way to get up close and personal with this magnificent order of birds!

🌲 Pick up the best pair of binoculars you can get. Littles are naturally a bit near-sighted, so they would benefit more from this than you might expect.

🌲 Get involved with the Audubon Society (audubon.org), especially if they are active in your area. You can access their conservation activities and be involved locally in learning and conserving. They even have summer and nature camps if you live in just the right place! Check out their website for more information.

🌲 Look for a "house window nesting box" on Amazon! How amazing to have a family of birds build a nest right in your window so that you can witness their entire process!

🌲 Don't forget- chickens are birds! If you don't have a backyard brood, a good friend may. Kids absolutely treasure the experience of gathering eggs and going through the process of either incubating (and watching them hatch, if fertilized) or cooking them up and eating them! (Green Eggs and Ham is a great fit for this!)

EVEN MORE FUN!

Activities: from Gentle + Classical Nature Term 1 Bundle
- Montessori 3-Part Cards
- French + Spanish Flashcards

☐ The website kids.nationalgeographic.com/animals has some AMAZING and engaging resources for children, including games and great facts to learn.

☐ The SQUILT music program is a favorite around here. They have a special collection of bird-inspired music, free to access. Find it here: http://bit.ly/squiltbird

☐ The most "required" project ever, related to birds, is to make your own homemade bird feeder. The standard idea is to get an old toilet paper roll, cover it in peanut butter, and roll it in seeds.

Hang it with yard somewhere that eager eyes can observe. And as always, Pinterest has a million other excellent bird feeder ideas and crafts!

- [ ] Nature's Playground (p46)

UNIT 8: FOREST ANIMALS

OVERVIEW

While we will focus more heavily on plant life in Terms 2 and 3 of GCN, you do have an opportunity here to go either way with this unit. For level 1 students, our memory focus is on forest animals. As we often do, we list a grouping to help our littles synthesize a "classification" in their mind of what animals call the forest their home. However, for level 2 students, I give the opportunity to discuss the 3 main types of forests. In level 3, you can go either way. I'll discuss this more in Teacher Notes. For the focus of this unit, I will use typical N. American forest animals, native to coniferous and deciduous forests. If you live local to a rainforest or boreal forest, feel free to make substitutions.

NATURE NUGGETS

https://www.zmescience.com/other/did-you-know/different-types-forests/

TEACHER NOTES

There are a few things to consider in advance for this unit. First, for a level 1 student, you could work on both a listing of animals and a short version of the level 2 statement ("There are 3 types of forests.") If you want your level 2 student to focus more on animals than on forest types, just have them use the level 1 statement instead. Level 3 will be a full-length combination of both.

As I mentioned in the unit overview, feel free to vary animals listed based on what's in your own backyard. A forest to me is not the same as a forest to my friends in Brazil :).

If you are working on your butterfly metamorphosis project this unit, save all your big explorations for next week. Unit 9 will be all about butterflies. However, one thing that I've always found beneficial is to have my children draw their own observations every couple of days, as they note changes in the size and behaviors of the caterpillars. They can essentially draw their own life cycle in this way!

Heads Up: When the pupa is ready to hatch, the shell will be transparent and you can see the dark colours of the butterfly's wings folded up inside. The transformation happens suddenly, and if you turn away for a few minutes, you will usually come back to find a butterfly.

In the Gentle + Classical Nature Bundle, you will find Forest Animal 3-Part Cards that are very helpful this unit.

UNIT 8 ATTAINMENTS

In this unit, we revisit our "Body of Water" for the term. Have you developed a system of working through observing and exploring different sections of your "Body of Water" yet? Or does your family prefer to follow their whims and dive deeply into various nooks and crannies haphazardly? There is no right way. The more you suit this exercise to your child's individual personality and learning style, the more of a lasting impression it will make.

Let's look back at our end "goal" from this exercise. The idea is that, when prompted, your child would have the enjoyment of closing their eyes and literally seeing the entire view of this special spot at once. He would be able to walk through the trails or along the bank, seeing the rippling water, watching the cattails bend, feeling the cool breeze, all in his mind. Under his own will, he can transport himself into this place time and again, throughout his entire life. He will have a collection of precious memories— of exploring, collecting, swimming, fishing— in this one special place, to share with his own children, just by closing his eyes.

Through this exercise of fully immersing and intentionally taking "snapshots" of moments and details and sensations, he is slowly and surely developing a full and deep awareness of his connection to God's Creation, and his place in this world. He will observe how his presence and actions affect this place he holds so dear. He will observe how the choices and behaviors of others either preserve or destroy even the smallest organism that calls this habitat home. He will observe the intricacies of the food webs and the delicacy of the biome in a way that a text book or living book could never sufficiently introduce. He will have gone knee-deep in experiencing the vast power of a Creator that could manifest such a living, breathing habitat as overwhelmingly diverse as the one he has come to know as his own.

As you visit this "Body of Water" and Walk/View again and again, both physically and in your minds' eyes, you and your child are developing keen observational skills, flexing the muscle of memory again and again, and developing a habit of attentiveness, alongside all of the incredible first-hand knowledge he is gaining as you drop well-timed and measured "seeds of truth" throughout your explorations. He is exercising his body with brisk activity, his will with habits of attention and obedience, his mind with new-found knowledge, and his soul with true wonder for a Creator who could orchestrate such majesty. There is no finer education!

This unit, we will revisit our Walk/View mentally as we have a "picture-painting" session. Remember to modify your technique as needed for your particular child. We want to balance pursuing new skills and abilities with not overwhelming or discouraging a struggling student.

I will encourage you that all students should continue to play any type or memory-building game that you might have, as the opportunity presents itself. One favorite family game that really builds visual memory muscles for level 2 and 3 students is QBits (found on Amazon). There is also a junior version for ages 3+. I also really like the Gifted Learning Flash Cards – Focus and Memory for Pre-K – Kindergarten (Amazon) for memory skills as well. I don't believe a child has to have a "bad" memory to utilize these tools either.

This is the last week of poem #2 for this term. If you don't have a poem chosen to recite and memorize for units 9-12, go ahead and select one now. There are beautiful poetry cards with related art included in the Term 1 Bundle, for your convenience.

In this unit, we are also adding the second wildflower that we will observe and collect (as well as draw/paint for older students). Once you know which flower you'd like to have your child learn about, you can gather it and include it in your Nature Collection Journal. On your nature explorations, try to keep an eye out for your two birds as well as your first tree and flower. Observe changes based on any weather alterations you had since you first identified these specimens. You can have your student notate these changes in their nature diary or collect updated specimens if you have a nature collection table or tray.

Unit 8 Attainment Goals
- [ ] Revisit Term 1 "Body of Water"; Continue to "picture-paint"
- [ ] Mentally review Term 1 Walk/View that you revisited last unit
- [ ] Select your second wildflower to observe and learn about. Review (in person or in the Nature Collection Journal) the tree, flower and birds you've observed so far
- [ ] Continue Term Project #2: Butterfly Metamorphosis
- [ ] Continue reciting your second poem of the term
- [ ] Continue daily practice of chosen handicraft

UNIT 8 AT-A-GLANCE

Unit 8 Attainment Goals
- ☐ Revisit Term 1 "Body of Water"; Continue to "picture-paint"
- ☐ Mentally review Term 1 Walk/View that you revisited last unit
- ☐ Select your second wildflower to observe and learn about. Review (in person or in the Nature Collection Journal) the tree, flower and birds you've observed so far
- ☐ Continue Term Project #2: Butterfly Metamorphosis
- ☐ Continue reciting your second poem of the term
- ☐ Continue daily practice of chosen handicraft

FOREIGN LANGUAGE

SPANISH	FRENCH
tree- el arbol	tree- l'arbre
forest- el bosque	forest- la fôret
leaf- la hoja	leaf- la feuille

MEMORY STATEMENTS

LEVEL 1	LEVEL 2	LEVEL 3
Deer, skunks, bears, and wolves are (temperate) forest animals.	The 3 types of forests are tropical, temperate, and boreal.	The 3 types of forests are tropical, temperate, and boreal. Deer, skunks, bears, and wolves are (temperate) forest animals.

LITERATURE SELECTIONS

LEVEL 1

Term Reading 1: Frog & Toad Storybook Treasury (Lobel)- 22 pages per unit

Highly Recommended:
Up in the Garden, Down in the Dirt (Messner)
Over in the Forest (Berkes)*author has many excellent titles
Nature Anatomy (Rothman) (p99, 132, 136-141, 144-147, 154-155)

Optional Book Menu:
Tall, Tall Tree (Fredericks)
Forest Bright, Forest Night (Ward)
Forest Adventure (Milton)
Whose Tracks are These? (Nail)

LEVEL 2

Term 1 Reading: Among the Pond People (Pierson)- 16 Pages per unit/3-5 pages per day

Highly Recommended:
Same as Level 1 Reading

Optional Book Menu:
Annie and the Wild Animals (Brett)
Big Tracks, Little Tracks (Selsam)
The Bears on Hemlock Mountain (Dalgliesh)
In the Snow: Who's Been Here? (George)
In the Woods: Who's Been Here? (George)
The Burgess Animal Book for Children (Burgess)
The Complete Brambly Hedge (Barklem)
Winnie-the-Pooh (Milne) *any of these

ACTIVITIES + FIELD TRIPS + EXPLORATIONS

KEYS TO REMEMBER

"Every day, every hour, the parents are either actively or passively forming those habits in their children upon which, more than upon anything else, future character and conduct depend." -Charlotte Mason (v1; p118)

"The first essential for the child's development is concentration." -Dr. Maria Montessori

FOREST ANIMAL EXPLORATIONS

🌲 Visit a local forest or park! While it's (maybe?) unlikely you would see any larger mammals, you can often see smaller forest animals and spot tracks of larger ones.

🌲 If your family has never camped or visited a forest for much time, could you swing a weekend camping trip? You might consider a cabin in the woods, if sleeping bags aren't your thing.

🌲 One way we get up-close and personal with forest animals is via the natural history museum attached to our zoo. There are many hands-on exhibits so that little ones can explore the various types of fur for themselves. Look for something similar in your area or via this link: http://bit.ly/NatMusUS

🌲 If you search "types of forests" on YouTube, it will yield several different, good videos. I would use this in addition to visiting your own local forest. Most of us won't get the opportunity to visit a tropical forest or boreal forest in person!

🌲 Find a list of national parks alongside specific activities for each state here: http://bit.ly/NatParks1

🌲 Be sure to take along a basket for collecting found objects while visiting your local forest. You can use these objects on your nature table, to decorate your home, or to sort through later. Have your children gather various items from each tree (branch, leaves, fruit/seed). Once at home, see if you can remember which fruit/seed went with which leaves, and so on. It's a great way to relive your fun day. You can also add these to your Nature Collection Journal and work to identify them.

EVEN MORE FUN!

Activities: from Gentle + Classical Nature Term 1 Bundle
- Montessori 3-Part Cards
- French + Spanish Flashcards
- Forest Habitat Poster

☐ After collecting leaves from the forest, press them into paint and make prints with them.

☐ Frame the leaves you collected on pretty black or white cardstock. They'll make gorgeous art!

☐ Create leaf rubbings by laying paper over the leaves and rubbing with chalk, charcoal, or a crayon. This will help your child see the veining more clearly.

☐ Nature's Playground (pg 126)

UNIT 9: INSECTS- BUTTERFLIES

OVERVIEW

If you started your butterfly project back around unit 7, you'll get to enjoy the culmination of that, soon. As I said before, I am always absolutely amazed at this transformation every time it happens. This unit, we really dive into learning more about butterflies beyond just experiencing this project.

HELPFUL NOTE: If you aren't currently doing the butterfly project due to weather/time of year, then one consideration might be to swap units 9 and 12. In unit 12, we study worms. Each unit's Nature Focus has been created to "stand alone" which gives you the flexibility to move any unit around. You definitely don't have to keep them in the order presented. Our ATTAINMENTS are the portion that build upon one another and can't easily be rearranged. Feel free to swap Nature Focus units but continue with Attainments as outlined.

NATURE NUGGETS

http://www.sciencekids.co.nz/sciencefacts/animals/butterfly.html
https://www.coolkidfacts.com/butterfly-facts/

TEACHER NOTES

For a few weeks, we've discussed the butterfly project. However, in the unit overview, I noted that if the weather isn't appropriate for that, to consider swapping units 9 and 12. Unit 12 focuses on worms. One super-interesting family project that you might consider would be either a worm farm/bin. In the event that you have decided not to do a butterfly project for any reason, you can find instructions on worm farms here: http://bit.ly/wormfarm1 Or, just like with the butterfly project, you can get all you need in a kit on Amazon (search "worm farm" in Biology Science Kits).

We are in the last quarter of Term 1, so it's time to select a NEW nature poem. Hopefully, your kids are able to memorize their poem via daily recitation. If they aren't, you can consider sticking with one poem longer or choosing a shorter poem.

In levels 2 and 3, we learn the term metamorphosis. You have an opportunity here to note how in unit 1, the process that tadpoles undergo to become frogs is called metamorphosis. The same goes for dragonflies in unit 3. Your kids will also find it interesting to note which animals undergo metamorphosis and which do not. Most insects and amphibians go through complete or incomplete metamorphosis. Mammals, fish, reptiles, and birds do not. This would be a great opportunity to sort the 3-Part Montessori cards based on metamorphosis/not.

Heads Up: Next unit we will explore a different insect: BEES! Bees are incredibly important and interesting. It would be a great unit to spread out for a little longer than normal. There are so many excellent books and projects- there's no need to rush through. Go ahead and consider/plan in advance a potential field trip to visit hives or view honey extraction, if available in your area.

In the Gentle + Classical Nature Bundle, you will find Insect 3-Part Cards and the French/Spanish Flashcards.

UNIT 9 ATTAINMENTS

We have TWO visits each left for the Walk/View and "Body of Water" this term. That means that as you revisit your Walk/View this unit, you'll want to really spend some time "picture-painting" areas that you may have overlooked or aren't quite sticking. Keep in mind that the goal is NOT absolute perfection. We do want to encourage completeness, attentiveness, and accuracy. Those are habits that we are cultivating through this exercise, but always (always) with grace.

One opportunity for discussion this week would be to hypothesize how different events could impact this Walk/View. Since you've likely been observing small (or large) changes to this habitat based on human interaction with it, you can use the information you've already gathered to make an educated guess about how other events might impact this area as well. What if there was even more garbage strewn? What if chemicals were disposed of nearby? What if chemicals were disposed of several miles away? What if air pollution became a problem? What if an invasive (or non-native) species was introduced? How might these different events impact the food web and health of the plants in the area?

If there is already an issue with pollution, could you organize an effort to educate your community or clean the area? Would other local homeschoolers want to band together to pick up debris and "adopt" this Walk/View? How might your choices now make a difference for this space in years to come?

This unit, you will also want to mentally review your "Body of Water." You could also consider having your child do a more in-depth project here as well.
- [ ] Would they like to create a scrapbook of images they've taken or draw their space themselves (sketch, brushdraw, watercolor, etc)?
- [ ] They could create a tri-fold display to share all they've learned and observed with family and friends. You might also consider a "Term Party" and invite extended family or friends to participate. Your children could choose a poem to recite, share a selection of memory work, display their drawings, collections, pictures, or any other work they've produced during the term as well.
- [ ] This can also be a party that you have just for your immediate family- to share with one another, in recap, all that you've learned and experienced.

In this unit, we are also adding our second tree that we will observe and collect (as well as draw/paint for older students). Once you know which tree you'd like to have your child learn about, you can gather it and include it in your <u>Nature Collection Journal</u>. On your nature explorations, try to keep an eye out for your two birds as well as your first tree and first and second flower. Observe changes based on any weather alterations you had since you first identified these specimens. You can have your student notate these changes in their nature diary or collect updated specimens if you have a nature collection table or tray.

Unit 9 Attainment Goals

- [ ] Revisit Term 1 Walk/View; Continue to "picture-paint"
- [ ] Mentally review Term 1 "Body of Water" that you revisited last unit
- [ ] Select your second tree to observe and learn about. Review (in person or in the Nature Collection Journal) the tree, flowers, and birds observed so far
- [ ] Continue Term Project #2: Butterfly Metamorphosis (or substitute Worm Farm)
- [ ] Begin reciting your third poem of the term
- [ ] Continue daily practice of chosen handicraft

UNIT 9 AT-A-GLANCE

Unit 9 Attainment Goals
- Revisit Term 1 Walk/View; Continue to "picture-paint"
- Mentally review Term 1 "Body of Water" that you revisited last unit
- Select your second tree to observe and learn about. Review (in person or in the Nature Collection Journal) the tree, flowers, and birds observed so far
- Continue Term Project #2: Butterfly Metamorphosis (or substitute Worm Farm)
- Begin reciting your third poem of the term
- Continue daily practice of chosen handicraft

FOREIGN LANGUAGE

SPANISH	FRENCH
caterpillar- la oruga	caterpillar- la chenille
butterfly- la mariposa	butterfly- le papillon
flower- la flor	flower- la fleur

MEMORY STATEMENTS

LEVEL 1	LEVEL 2	LEVEL 3
Caterpillars turn into chrysalises then into butterflies.	Butterfly metamorphosis has 4 stages: egg, caterpillar, chrysalis, butterfly	Metamorphosis is the process of changing from one form into another and includes 4 stages for butterflies: egg, caterpillar, chrysalis, butterfly.

LITERATURE SELECTIONS

LEVEL 1

Term Reading 1: Frog & Toad Storybook Treasury (Lobel)- 22 pages per unit

Highly Recommended:
Up in the Garden, Down in the Dirt (Messner)
Nature Anatomy (Rothman) (p70-81)

Optional Book Menu:
The Busy Tree (Ward)
In the Tall, Tall Grass (Fleming)
The Very Hungry Caterpillar (Carle)
Where Butterflies Grow (Ryder)
A Butterfly is Patient (Aston)
Monarch and Milkweed (Frost)
Are You a Butterfly? (Allen)

LEVEL 2

Term 1 Reading: Among the Pond People (Pierson)- 16 Pages per unit/3-5 pages per day

Highly Recommended:
Same as Level 1 Reading

Optional Book Menu:
Monarch Butterfly (Gibbons)
Velma Gratch & the Way Cool Butterfly (Madison)
Gotta Go! Gotta Go! (Swope) *early reader
Small Wonders (Smith) *Jean-Heri Fabre Bio
Caterpillars, Bugs, & Butterflies: Take-Along Guide (Boring)
The Big Book of Bugs (Zommer)

ACTIVITIES + FIELD TRIPS + EXPLORATIONS

KEYS TO REMEMBER

"We are all meant to be naturalists, each in his own degree, and it's inexcusable to live in a world so full of marvels of plants and animal life and to care for none of these things." -Charlotte Mason

"The things he sees are not just remembered; they form a part of his soul." -Dr. Maria Montessori

BUTTERFLY EXPLORATIONS

🌲 If you are doing the butterfly project, this is probably the absolute best way to really understand the life cycles and needs of a butterfly. Observe them daily (though you likely won't have to remind your child).

🌲 Many botanical gardens, natural history museums, zoos, herpetology exhibits, and even aquariums have spaces for butterfly encounters. A quick Google will help you find one in your state (or ask in your local homeschool Facebook group). If possible, I encourage you to arrange a guided field trip (and invite a few other homeschool families along).

🌲 Plant a butterfly garden! What an incredible way to nurture the environment and bring a variety of gorgeous butterflies right to your own door. Even if you live in an apartment in a city, you could still do a small window planter, as long as you have some access to an outdoor space. Amazon (and of course your local garden center) will sell seed selections specifically designed to attract butterflies (and bees, which is great for the next unit).

🌲 I've also seen small butterfly feeders available which are very similar to hummingbird feeders as well as butterfly houses. I've not used them but they look very intriguing!

EVEN MORE FUN!

Activities: from Gentle + Classical Nature Term 1 Bundle
- Montessori 3-Part Cards
- French + Spanish Flashcards
- Butterfly Life Cycle Poster and Worksheet

📖 I've seen several cute ideas on Pinterest if you love crafts: Clothespins + Tissue= Butterfly, Using clear contact paper + tissue paper= Butterfly; plus a slew of "Very Hungry Caterpillar"-inspired crafts.

📖 Nature's Playground (p140)

UNIT 10: INSECTS- BEES

OVERVIEW

Wonderful bees! Bees have gotten a lot of attention over the last few years- and rightfully so. They are imperative to our survival, extremely fascinating, make the most delicious and healthy treat, AND are dying off in record numbers. Depending upon your child's age and sensitivity, that last point might or might not be explored too deeply. In our Nature Focus, we will be learning specifically about honeybees and the types of bees that colonize their hive.

NATURE NUGGETS

https://www.natgeokids.com/au/discover/animals/insects/honey-bees/

TEACHER NOTES

I've chosen a short menu of book suggestions on the "At-a-Glance" page as usual, but please know there are countless excellent books that discuss this topic from either the perspective of how bees live and make honey to their significance to our environment and food chain. I think approaching the topic from both perspectives is excellent and gives a well-rounded perspective. Your kids won't likely look the same at a bee floating by again! You'll find both kinds of books recommended in the menu.

I became familiar with Nature Nate's honey via Instagram last year. As a brand ambassador, they sent me a t-shirt and samples along with their story. After learning more about their sustainability practices, why that's so important, and their overall (Christian) philosophy of how they do business and steward resources, you won't soon find me using any other brand of honey (except for that from local farmers). You can learn more about Nature Nate's philosophies, key information about bee conservation, and get their free ebook on the topic here: naturenates.com/long-live-the-bees/   They also have a free lesson plan with printables here: naturenates.com/teachers-free-lesson-plans/

Looking forward: There are only 2 units left in Term 1 of Gentle + Classical Nature. Next up, we will shift from insects to arachnids and learn all about our 8-legged friends. We wind up this term with a look at worms! I mentioned last unit that doing a worm farm is an option in leiu of the butterfly project, but I would also like to suggest that everyone try their hand at composting and creating a worm farm in that last unit! While our goal is 2 projects per term, creating a maintaining a worm bin (or compost bin) is a FANTASTIC way to learn not just about worms and their part in our food chain and environment, but about decomposition in general.

In the Gentle + Classical Nature Bundle, you will find Insect 3-Part Cards that are very helpful this unit. You'll also find your French/Spanish Flashcards, a Bee Life Cycle poster, and a Butterfly Life Cycle sheet for your metamorphosis project.

Worship Point: The 4-part life cycle that many of God's creatures experience mirrors the same process we walk through as new creations in Christ. These animals begin as the smallest creation, but go through a variety of internal and external changes- often shedding off their former selves to be made into something completely new and different. This is a perfect metaphor for our children to understand how WE are made new in Christ as believers. Once was once an unattractive grubby caterpillar or larva ends up being a beautiful butterfly or an industrious and important bee. There are so many parallels to explore as your disciple your children!

UNIT 10 ATTAINMENTS

We have TWO visits left for our "Body of Water" this term and one more for our Walk/View. This process of visiting, observing, and remembering may have gone gloriously for you, or you may have felt like an utter failure. Your child might have a memory like a steel trap or may barely remember that you even go on nature walks. He might love the out-of-doors and never want to leave, or he may have a tantrum to have to go outside each day. I say all of this to say: **You aren't alone**. Every child is different, but it's most likely that your child is not some odd anomaly. They all have natural abilities that they excel at that need little encouragement from us... and they all have natural weaknesses and areas of sin that we must not run from.

If your child doesn't enjoy the places you visit, or going outside, or practicing attentiveness and memorization, that's OK. But let me encourage you— that doesn't mean you quit. I've been a parent for just a decade and a half, but one thing that I've learned most thoroughly is that we cannot run from hard things. Because, as home educators, we want to create an education that's specifically designed for our child's learning style and abilities, we often get confused and believe that our child must LIKE and ENJOY their education to benefit from it... that if they don't like their work, we must be doing it wrong and we must change course.

I want to take the time to encourage you that the greatest character gains and increases in ability you'll likely ever see in your child are the ones found after you stayed the course— the really, really hard course. Growth is never easy. Character is not created by accident. If habit is worth 10 natures, then as mothers, we must have the habit of not failing to persevere in habit formation in our children. That means consistency, even when they don't care for the thing. Sometimes, we are off mark and need to choose a different route. But oftentimes, when things have gotten challenging and we are tiring of rebellion and battles, we must buckle down all the more and encourage them to push forward. They will reap no greater benefit in their education than the ability to do things that are truly hard and to overcome challenges with success— courage instilled and weaknesses improved.

This unit, you will mentally review your Walk/View before visiting it for the last time next unit (or obviously, last time per this curriculum). Continue to persist as you've been doing... slowly leading your child toward these skills with gentle persistence, encouraging and loving all the way. If your child never really got to the point of "picture-painting" and has been doing exercises building slowly toward that goal, EXCELLENT! This is absolutely not a sprint, but a marathon. Keep persisting. Feel free to circle back through the attainments again.

In this unit, we don't add to our collections, but still review and revisit our 2 birds, 2 trees, and 2 flowers. Use your wisdom in knowing when to review via the <u>Nature Collection Journal</u> or your nature table vs when a visit to your tree and flower would be in order. Also, don't forget about the game of sight-seeing detailed on page 34 where you task your children to "go and see" and come back, detailing all they observed with accuracy. You can employ those same games with flowers, trees, and birds.

Unit 10 Attainment Goals
- [ ] Revisit Term 1 "Body of Water"; Continue to "picture-paint"
- [ ] Mentally review Term 1 Walk/View that you revisited last unit
- [ ] Review (in person or in the <u>Nature Collection Journal</u>) the two trees, birds, and flowers you've observed so far
- [ ] Continue Term Project #2: Butterfly Metamorphosis (or substitute Worm Farm)
- [ ] Continue reciting your third poem of the term
- [ ] Continue daily practice of chosen handicraft

UNIT 10 AT-A-GLANCE

Unit 10 Attainment Goals

- ☐ Revisit Term 1 "Body of Water"; Continue to "picture-paint"
- ☐ Mentally review Term 1 Walk/View that you revisited last unit
- ☐ Review (in person or in the Nature Collection Journal) the two trees, birds, and flowers you've observed so far
- ☐ Continue Term Project #2: Butterfly Metamorphosis (or substitute Worm Farm)
- ☐ Continue reciting your third poem of the term
- ☐ Continue daily practice of chosen handicraft

FOREIGN LANGUAGE

SPANISH	FRENCH
bee- la abeja	bee- l'abeille
honey- la miel	honey- la miel
pollen- el polen	pollen- le pollen

MEMORY STATEMENTS

LEVEL 1	LEVEL 2	LEVEL 3
Honeybees make honey from the nectar of flowers.	There are three types of bees in a honeybee hive: queen, workers, and drones.	Bees transfer pollen between the male and female parts of flowers, allowing plants to grow seeds and fruit. (PLUS Level 2)

LITERATURE SELECTIONS

LEVEL 1

Term Reading 1: Frog & Toad Storybook Treasury (Lobel)- 22 pages per unit

Highly Recommended:
Up in the Garden, Down in the Dirt (Messner)
Nature Anatomy (Rothman) (p70-81)

Optional Book Menu:
Bee: A Peek-Through Picture Book (Teckentrup)
Bee & Me (Jay)
The Honeybee (Hall)
Are You a Bee? (Allen)
The Honey Makers (Gibbons)
Five Bizzy Honeybees (Douglas)

LEVEL 2

Term 1 Reading: Among the Pond People (Pierson)- 16 Pages per unit/3-5 pages per day

Highly Recommended:
Same as Level 1 Reading

Optional Book Menu:
Bees- A Honeyed History (Socha)
Flight of the Honeybee (Huber)
The Bee Tree (Pollaco)
The Life & Times of a Honeybee (Mucicci)
The Honeybee Man (Nargi)
What if there were no bees? (Slade)
The Bee Book (Milner)

ACTIVITIES + FIELD TRIPS + EXPLORATIONS

KEYS TO REMEMBER

Kind words are like honey--sweet to the soul and healthy for the body. -Proverbs 16:24

"It cannot be too often said that information is not education." -Charlotte Mason

BEE EXPLORATIONS

🌲 Find a local beekeeper! You won't find anyone as knowledgeable or passionate about bee health, conservation, and delicious honey. Beekeepers are fascinating to talk to and there's likely no field trip that your children will more clearly remember. This website will be a good starting place to find one in your area (though, local Facebook groups are helpful too): www.beeculture.com/find-local-beekeeper/

🌲 It's entirely un-CM, but we love the movie "The Bee Movie." It has a great story, is humorously insightful, and the whole story comes down to the importance of bees to the earth's plant and animal life.

🌲 Perform a family honey taste-testing. Buy a variety of different honey brands, local and national. Be sure to get some raw/unfiltered and some filtered. Have a taste-testing to find a family favorite. Can you tell the different between local/national or pasteurized/raw?

🌲 Search "bee hotel" on Pinterest to find a variety of methods of creating your own. (In general, bug hotels are pretty cool and there are a variety of plans and methods on Pinterest.) You can also find these on Amazon.

EVEN MORE FUN!

Activities: from Gentle + Classical Nature Term 1 Bundle
- Montessori 3-Part Cards
- French + Spanish Flashcards
- Butterfly Life Cycle Poster
- Bee Life Cycle Poster

♪ Flight of the Bumblebee - Rimsky-Korsakov is a must-listen this week!
♪ Buy sheets of beeswax to roll into beeswax candles- no dipping or heat required!
♪ Also consider making beeswax poured candles or soaps with your level 2+ children

📋 Nature's Playground (pg 98)

UNIT 11: ARACHNIDS- SPIDERS

OVERVIEW

This may not be your favorite unit. I won't argue with you. But as we travel from the depths of the pond, up into the sky and down into the forest, we simply can't skip over the amazing creativity of God in these masterpieces. They are incredibly integral to our world's ecosystems and as diverse as insects in their appearance and purposes. You can classify these next two units as "things you find under a log."

NATURE NUGGETS

http://www.sciencekids.co.nz/sciencefacts/animals/spider.html

https://easyscienceforkids.com/all-about-arachnids/

TEACHER NOTES

Spiders are super interesting and simultaneously super-creepy. Most of us just scream and run, but I love this quote from Charlotte Mason on this topic:

"Children should be encouraged to watch, patiently and quietly, until they learn something of the habits and history of bee, ant, wasp, spider, hairy caterpillar, dragon-fly, and whatever of larger growth comes in their way.... With regard to the horror which some children show of beetle, spider, worm, that is usually a trick picked up from grown-up people. Kingsley's children would run after their 'daddy' with a 'delicious worm,' a 'lovely toad,' a 'sweet beetle' carried tenderly in both hands. There are real antipathies not to be overcome, such as Kingsley's own horror of a spider; but children who are accustomed to hold and admire caterpillars and beetles from their babyhood will not give way to affected horrors. The child who spends an hour in watching the ways of some new 'grub' he has come upon will be a man of mark yet." (v1; p58-59)

That's a convicting encouragement for not setting a poor example of being frightened of "all the things." As noted in the Nature Nugget links, there are only 2 types of poisonous spiders in the US, but multiple species. They all belong to the Widow or Recluse families. It's smart to research which species live in your area, the type of habitat they usually occupy, and any identifying marks. (Or research poisonous spiders native to your particular area). When in doubt, don't touch. You might even take along some thick kitchen gloves if you intend to flip over any logs on a Nature Exploration (which I highly encourage!). The life under and inside of a rotting log is a perfect little biome that houses a huge variety of mollusks, insects, arachnids, and worms.

Next unit is our last unit of Term 1. In it we will explore worms and their habitats, so it's very easy to blend some of Units 11 and 12 together. However, spiders have a much broader variety of places they call "home" than worms do.

©Gentle + Classical Nature

If your butterfly project has come to an end, I encourage you to consider an optional third project for the term, as mentioned last unit: a worm farm! You can completely create one DIY in a 5 gallon bucket or find a kit on Amazon. You can make it as simple or complex as you'd like. Worm farms are very low-maintenance as well and are a great way to dispose of newspapers and kitchen waste. They make a phenomenal study of decomposition! We are in the middle of turning an old roadside refrigerator find into a large worm farm for fishing bait! Here's the link on how to DIY one again: http://bit.ly/wormfarm1

UNIT 11 ATTAINMENTS

This is our last term-assigned visit to our Walk/View! I would encourage you to make this visit extra special. Stay longer than normal, bring special treats, pick up trash, explore the last unexplored areas, invite friends along to see this special space you've been growing so closely acquainted with. I especially love the idea of having your child paint the "picture" of this Walk/View for a family member then having them come see for themselves! What a special treat!

You'll also mentally revisit your "Body of Water" before going to it for the last time next unit. I hope that you've come to love and have a deep connection to both of these places. I hope your sweet children (and you, Mama!) have developed a love for the sights, sounds, smells, sensations, and memories of these venues that will last a life time!

Looking ahead: In Term 2, you will cycle through a new Walk/View and "Body of Water." If your local resources are limited, feel free to stick with the current ones longterm. There's no RULE that says you absolutely must have 3 Walk/Views and 3 "Bodies of Water." If you feel like more time is needed at these locations, make that adjustment as well. The beauty in homeschooling is that we can follow our specific passions and needs.

In this unit, we add to our Nature Collection Journal with our third wildflower. Several weeks have passed since you chose your first wildflower. Try to visit its location and see what has changed. Also, review and revisit your 2 birds, 2 trees, and 2 flowers you've chosen thus far. Use your wisdom in knowing when to review via the Nature Collection Journal or your nature table vs when a visit to your tree and flower would be in order. Also, don't forget about the game of sight-seeing detailed on page 34 where you task your children to "go and see" and come back, detailing all they observed with accuracy. You can employ those same games with flowers, trees, and birds.

Unit 11 Attainment Goals
- [ ] Revisit Term 1 Walk/View for the last time; Continue to "picture-paint"
- [ ] Mentally review Term 1 "Body of Water" that you revisited last unit
- [ ] Collect your 3rd wildflower and mount in Nature Collection Journal
- [ ] Review (in person or in the Nature Collection Journal) the two trees, birds, and flowers you've observed so far
- [ ] Continue/Finish Term Project #2: Butterfly Metamorphosis. Consider a third project: Worm Farm
- [ ] Continue reciting your third poem of the term
- [ ] Continue daily practice of chosen handicraft

UNIT 11 AT-A-GLANCE

Unit 11 Attainment Goals
- ☐ Revisit Term 1 Walk/View for the last time, Continue to "picture-paint"
- ☐ Mentally review Term 1 "Body of Water" that you revisited last unit
- ☐ Collect your 3rd wildflower and mount in Nature Collection Journal
- ☐ Review (in person or in the Nature Collection Journal) the two trees, birds, and flowers you've observed so far
- ☐ Continue/Finish Term Project #2: Butterfly Metamorphosis. Consider a third project: Worm Farm
- ☐ Continue reciting your third poem of the term
- ☐ Continue daily practice of chosen handicraft

FOREIGN LANGUAGE

SPANISH	FRENCH
spider- la araña	spider- l'araignee
leg- la pierna	leg- la jambe
eight- ocho	eight- huit

MEMORY STATEMENTS

LEVEL 1	LEVEL 2	LEVEL 3
Arachnids are arthropods with 8 legs.	Spiders, scorpions, and ticks are all arachnids.	Spiders, scorpions, and ticks are all arachnids, have 8 legs, no antenna, and 2 body sections.

LITERATURE SELECTIONS

LEVEL 1
Term Reading 1: Frog & Toad Storybook Treasury (Lobel)- 22 pages per unit

Highly Recommended:
Up in the Garden, Down in the Dirt (Messner)
Nature Anatomy (Rothman) (p92-93)

Optional Book Menu:
The Very Busy Spider (Carle)
A House Spider's Life (Himmelman)
Sophie's Masterpiece (Spinelli)
Spiders (Gibbons)
Are You a Spider? (Allen)
One Small Place in a Tree (Brenner)

LEVEL 2
Term 1 Reading: Among the Pond People (Pierson)- 16 Pages per unit/3-5 pages per day

Highly Recommended:
Same as Level 1 Reading

Optional Book Menu:
Charlotte's Web (White)
Be Nice to Spiders (Graham)
Diary of a Spider (Cronin)
I'm Trying to Love Spiders (Barton) *silly
Nefertiti: The Spidernaut (Pattison) *very cool story

ACTIVITIES + FIELD TRIPS + EXPLORATIONS

KEYS TO REMEMBER

Be cautious and informed about spider exploration, but try not to set the example of being frightened or grossed out by all spiders.

"Point to some loverly flower or gracious tree, not only as a beautiful work, but a beautiful thought of God." -Charlotte Mason (v1; p80)

SPIDER EXPLORATIONS

🌲 Make sure to use your 3-Part Montessori Cards for sorting: Sort insects from arachnids and add some math skills by counting legs when in doubt. You can also sort by environment as well (which ones live underneath a rock or old tree?)

🌲 Does your zoo have a special arachnid exhibit? Does your local university have an entomology department that you could visit to learn from a professional? While entomologists study insects, many of them also study the arachnids and other arthropods as well. Consider checking with your local pest control specialists; do they provide any educational/conservation related resources?

🌲 In our area, spiders come out at dusk and begin weaving enormous looms to catch a midnight snack. Try an after-dark excursion, flashlight in hand, to see if you can find a big garden spider in action. Watching a spider weave a web in person is truly breathtaking!

🌲 Make a "bug guts" smoothie! Spiders inject poison into their pray, liquefying them, and then ingest them that way. If you have a kid who that doesn't totally gross out, maybe a green "bug guts" smoothie is in order?

🌲 Finger-knitting would be a great way to help your little ones "feel like" a spider!

EVEN MORE FUN!

Activities: from Gentle + Classical Nature Term 1 Bundle
- Montessori 3-Part Cards
- French + Spanish Flashcards

📋 If you have a good assortment of Toob animals (especially insects and spiders), sorting those to match the Montessori 3-Part Cards is always a fun, educational experience.

📋 Use an Oreo, 8 pretzels, some icing, and mini-M&Ms to make a spider. (Oreo body, covered in some icing, add 8 eyes, and 8 pretzel legs).

📋 Sing "Itsy-Bitsy-Spider." We have a board book version that my boys LOVE to read about Itsy's creativity in finding another way up the water spout! (by Kate Toms)

📋 Pinterest is FULL of crafty spider ideas: Make a spider from a paper plate by attaching pipe cleaners or construction paper legs, make a spider hat, or create a web from a paper plate with string.

📋 Nature's Playground (pg 110)

UNIT 12: WORMS

OVERVIEW

How exciting! You have made it to the end of Term 1: Inland Waterways and Forests of Gentle + Classical Nature! Whether it took you 12 quick weeks or you meandered through each unit slowly over several months, I hope you've been blessed. I also hope you'll enjoy Term 2: Coastal Woodlands and Oceans (later fall 2019) and Term 3: Down on the Farm and Around the World (winter 2019)!

This unit, I hope you'll consider doing a small worm farm or a few of the suggested activities to observe worms and decomposition in action. As a matter of fact, these two areas are so closely related that I'm sharing both worm and decomposition link in Nature Nuggets. It's hard to study these little guys without learning about their important function. Feel free to focus in more on the worms or on their jobs, or take time to sift through both topics. Furthermore, while there are 3000+ species of worms, we will be focusing in on earthworms this unit.

NATURE NUGGETS

https://kidsgrowingstrong.org/worms/

http://bit.ly/decomposers1

TEACHER NOTES

I would highly encourage you to check out the links I've referenced right above. (Don't forget you can find the clickable versions at www.GentleClassical.com.) Even if your kids don't watch the videos with you, they'll help you feel fully equipped to share amazing facts about the process that worms work through that both break down waste and create fertile ground for growing new plant life. It's an amazing life cycle that benefits us all very directly. The impact of proper soil will be further investigated in Term 3: Down on the Farm and Around the World.

If you happen to finish up Term 1 rather quickly, before Term 2 has been released, please feel free to cycle back through some of your favorite units you've touched on. You can also spend a few weeks practicing and reviewing your memory work and foreign language terms. I also highly encourage you to consider a "Term Party" where your students share their projects, field trip pictures, and new knowledge along with possibly a "science fair" type display for special family members or friends. Children are always so encouraged to realize that the information they've been working hard to gain is not "just for school" or "just for them." Their extended family, church family, or friends would love to glean from all of their hard work. Making the completion of this term a "big deal" will get them very excited to keep moving forward!

Reminder: If your butterfly project has come to an end, I encourage you to consider an optional third project for the term, as mentioned last unit: a worm farm! Worm farms are super low-maintenance as well and are a great way to dispose of newspapers and kitchen waste. http://bit.ly/wormfarm1

UNIT 12 ATTAINMENTS

This is our last official visit to our special "Body of Water!" I hope that you and your children have grown intimately knowledgeable about this special place you chose. I hope you've grown closer as a family and have grown intricately aware of the magnificence of our incredible God who knit every aspect you observed together, by simply speaking it into existence. Isn't God amazing!?! You'll also want to take one last "mental walk" through your Walk/View.

Reminder: In Term 2, you will cycle through a new Walk/View and "Body of Water." If your local resources are limited, feel free to stick with your current ones longterm. There's no RULE that says you absolutely must have 3 Walk/Views and 3 "Bodies of Water."

In this unit, we add to our Nature Collection Journal with our fourth wildflower. Don't forget to visit and revisit your two trees, two birds, and now 4 wildflowers as often as possible- noting their seasonal changes and cycles.

Unit 12 Attainment Goals
- [ ] Revisit Term 1 "Body of Water" for the last time; Continue to "picture-paint"
- [ ] Mentally review Term 1 Walk/View that you revisited last unit
- [ ] Collect your 4th wildflower and mount in Nature Collection Journal
- [ ] Review (in person or in the Nature Collection Journal) the trees, birds, and flowers you've observed so far
- [ ] Continue/Finish Term Project #2: Butterfly Metamorphosis. Consider a third project: Worm Farm
- [ ] Continue reciting your third poem of the term
- [ ] Continue daily practice of chosen handicraft

UNIT 12 AT-A-GLANCE

Unit 12 Attainment Goals
- ☐ Revisit Term 1 "Body of Water" for the last time; Continue to "picture-paint"
- ☐ Mentally review Term 1 Walk/View that you revisited last unit
- ☐ Collect your 4th wildflower and mount in Nature Collection Journal
- ☐ Review (in person or in the Nature Collection Journal) the trees, birds, and flowers you've observed so far
- ☐ Continue/Finish Term Project #2: Butterfly Metamorphosis. Consider a third project: Worm Farm
- ☐ Continue reciting your third poem of the term
- ☐ Continue daily practice of chosen handicraft

FOREIGN LANGUAGE

SPANISH	FRENCH
worm- la lombriz	worm- la vere de terre
soil- el tierra	soil- la terre
eye- el ojo	eye- l'oeil

MEMORY STATEMENTS

LEVEL 1	LEVEL 2	LEVEL 3
Earthworms help to make our soil healthy.	Earthworms have no eyes, ears, or bones and breathe through their skin.	Earthworms are ectotherms that have no eyes, ears, or bones and play a significant role in the food chain as decomposers.

LITERATURE SELECTIONS

LEVEL 1
Term Reading 1: Frog & Toad Storybook Treasury (Lobel)- 22 pages per unit

Highly Recommended:
Up in the Garden, Down in the Dirt (Messner)
Nature Anatomy (Rothman) (p126-127)

Optional Book Menu:
Wonderful Worms (Glases)
Worm Weather (Taft)
An Earthworm's Life (Himmelman)
Compost Stew (Siddals)
underGROUND (Fleming)

LEVEL 2
Term 1 Reading: Among the Pond People (Pierson)- 16 Pages per unit/3-5 pages per day

Highly Recommended:
Same as Level 1 Reading

Optional Book Menu:
Wiggling Worms at Work (Pfeffer)
Yucky Worms (French)
Diary of a Worm (Cronin)
Garden Wigglers (Lowen)
Composting: Nature's Recyclers (Koontz)

ACTIVITIES + FIELD TRIPS + EXPLORATIONS

KEYS TO REMEMBER

"Danger lurks in the Kindergarten, just in proportion to the completeness and beauty of its organisation. It is possible to supplement Nature so skillfully that we run some risk of supplanting her, depriving her of space and time to do her own work in her own way. 'Go and see what Tommy is doing and tell him he mustn't,' is not sound doctrine. Tommy should be free to do what he likes with his limbs and his mind through all the hours of the day when he is not sitting up nicely at meals. He should run and jump, leap and tumble, lie on his face watching a worm, or on his back watching the bees in a lime tree. Nature will look after him and give him promptings of desire to know many things; and somebody must tell as he wants to know; and to do many things, and somebody should be handy just to put him in the way; and to be many things, naughty and good, and somebody should give direction." -Charlotte Mason (v1; p192-193)

From one mother to another: If you struggle with frustration that your "Tommy" doesn't so well entertain himself out of doors as the Tommy in this quote, I want to encourage you to evaluate two things- screen time and a potential lack of insistence that "Tommy" entertain himself. In my own motherhood, I've found myself fallen trap to "keeping the children entertained" and thusly never allowing them boredom. This entertainment usually comes from structured activities, school at home, or screens. While all good (or OK) in very right proportions, often our children suffer from the inability to entertain their own mind with all that nature has to offer because we've spent too much time entertaining their minds for them. You'll likely walk a few days through some very rough complaining and cries of boredom, but urge them again and again to go play with *some suggestions* alone, and they'll soon find their complaining doesn't help. Modeling restful nature observation and interaction will inspire them to dig in alone as well.

WORM EXPLORATIONS

🌲 Dare I say- dissection? It's very commonplace for students to dissect an earthworm in schools. I'm personally not a fan of it (weak stomach here), especially in the early elementary years. However, if you have a particularly audacious child, this may be right up his alley!

🌲 Field trip to the bait shop! In Alabama, we have a fishing bait store every few miles. You can grab a whole tub of night crawlers or wigglers for just a few dollars. You can use these to begin your own worm farm or compost bin OR just to get up close and personal with these creatures.

🌲 Head outside after a good rain in the summertime and you may find quite a few little earthworms have made their way up to the surface. When we lived in a neighborhood, my girls would run outside to try to "rescue" these little guys from the forthcoming sunshine on the sidewalk.

🌲 Head out to one of your favorite (shadier) nature exploration spots. Look for a log or rock and take a careful peak underneath. You'll likely find a variety of little critters as well as their various holes they dig down into.

🚶 If you have a forest to visit, see if you can do a little digging to show your kids how the various layers on the forest floor cover one another up to create a decomposition sandwich. On top, you'll have whole fallen leaves, but as you slowly remove layer upon layer, you'll find leaves that are broken and chewed into smaller and smaller bits. You may even find a worm or two (or worm castings!). You'll eventually end up down in the rich, fertile soil.

EVEN MORE FUN!

<u>Activities</u>: from <u>Gentle + Classical Nature</u> Term 1 Bundle
- Montessori 3-Part Cards
- French + Spanish Flashcards

☐ Search "decomposition activity" on Pinterest to come up with some phenomenal additional ideas.

☐ <u>Nature's Playground</u>- (pg 144-145)

APPENDIX

HIGHLY RECOMMENDED RESOURCES + BOOKS

FOR MOM:
Volume 1: Home Education by Charlotte Mason
Nature's Playground by Fiona Danks and Jo Schofield (This books is referenced in the "Even More Fun" section each unit with additional, creative, and RICH outdoor activities.)
FREE Digital Version of ALL volumes from Charlotte Mason:
https://www.amblesideonline.org/CM/toc.html

SCIENCE SPINE:
Over and Under the Pond (Messner)
Up in the Garden, Down in the Dirt (Messner)
Nature Anatomy (Rothman)
Nature Collection Journal (Erin Cox from LifeAbundantlyBlog.com/shop)

TERM READ ALOUDS (NATURE LORE):
Frog and Toad Storybook Treasury (Lobel)
Among the Pond People (Pierson)
Substitute: Winnie-the-Pooh (Milne)

GENTLE + CLASSICAL NATURE BUNDLE FROM LIFE, ABUNDANTLY INCLUDES:

- Nature Collection Journal
- Printable Book Menu
- Printable Attainment Tracking List
- Printable "At-a-Glance" pages
- Formidable List of Attainments Poster
- Montessori 3-Part Cards (100 Cards Total)
- Menu of Handicrafts
- Memory Statement Cards (half page), Levels 1, 2, and 3
- French and Spanish Flashcards
- 1/2 Poetry Cards with Art (half page)
- Poetry Selections (Levels 1 and 2)
- Memory Statement Copywork (Levels 1 and 2)
- "Attainments this Unit" Board Sheets (half page)
- Bird Observation Pack
- Life Cycle Posters and Activities and MORE!

EXPANSION PACK (LEVEL 3 STUDENTS THROUGH 6TH GRADE)- **SOLD SEPARATELY FROM BUNDLE**
- Book Menu for Level 3 Readers/Listeners
- Copywork

- Level 3 Poetry Selections
- Poetry Cards
- Writing Prompts
- Projects

TRUSTED ADDITIONAL RESOURCES

Rooted Childhood for Handicraft Guidance and Suggestions (www.RootedChildhood.com)
<u>Usborne Picture Dictionary in French</u> (Brooks)
<u>Usborne Picture Dictionary in Spanish </u>(Brooks)

I have curated collections of excellent educational books for Mom, direct links for each recommended book in this program, as well as great "gear" for getting outside. You can see all of that by visiting www.GentleClassical.com

Visit www.GentleClassical.com and click "Helpful Tools" or "Shoppable Book Menu" to find a convenient listing of all suggested materials and books mentioned in this program.

"Body of Water" + Walk/View Notes to Consider

When choosing your "Body of Water" and Walk/View for each term, there are several important elements that you will want to keep in mind. The following is a list of suggested questions to ponder when making this decision:

Is this location convenient enough that I will enjoy visiting weekly or biweekly?
Will I need special permission to visit this property?
Will the "walk" be interesting enough to engage without being cumbersome to visit often?
Is it relatively free of modern alterations? (If you live in a highly urban area, do what you can! The PROCESS is the most important thing.)
Is it safe?
Is there any particular wildlife I need to be more educated about before visiting this area?
Is it pleasant? Is the view worthy of memory?

If you are coming up empty-handed, consider local parks, a nearby national park, a local farm, a favorite area at a local zoo or museum, a rooftop garden, or any garden (community or otherwise).

Ideally, your special locations would be both convenient and beautiful and brimming with nature to observe and explore. But, that may not always be the case. Do what you can with what you have! Even if it isn't as "idyllic" as you would like, this is YOUR city that you are exploring. This environment is the environment of your child's childhood. Look for beauty everywhere you go, focus on the skills we are aiming to attain, and trust God to take care of the rest!

Attainment Planning + Tracking

Walk/View Term 1: _____
Walk/View Term 2: _____
Walk/View Term 3: _____
"Body of Water" Term 1: _____
"Body of Water" Term 2: _____
"Body of Water" Term 3: _____

Term 1 Poems
Poem 1: _____
Poem 2: _____
Poem 3: _____

Term 2 Poems
Poem 1: _____
Poem 2: _____
Poem 3: _____

Term 3 Poems
Poem 1: _____
Poem 2: _____
Poem 3: _____

Term 1 Projects
Project 1: _____
Project 2: _____
Project 3: _____
*optional

Term 2 Projects
Project 1: _____
Project 2: _____
Project 3: _____
*optional

Term 3 Projects
Project 1: _____
Project 2: _____
Project 3: _____
*optional

Flower #1: _____
Flower #2: _____
Flower #3: _____
Flower #4: _____
Flower #5: _____
Flower #6: _____
Flower #7: _____
Flower #8: _____
Flower #9: _____
Flower #10: _____
Flower #11: _____
Flower #12: _____
Tree #1: _____
Tree #2: _____
Tree #3: _____
Tree #4: _____
Tree #5: _____
Tree #6: _____
Bird #1: _____
Bird #2: _____
Bird #3: _____
Bird #4: _____
Bird #5: _____
Bird #6: _____
Handicrafts
Term 1: _____
Term 2: _____
Term 3: _____

Coming Summer 2019

In Gentle + Classical Preschool Level 2, the remainder of Charlotte Mason's attainments will be explored and realized by students, all the while exploring art, music, literature, math, history, scripture and more! An excellent blend of Classical and CM philosophies!

Learn More: www.GentleClassical.com

Made in the USA
Middletown, DE
24 August 2019